Crisis Care
Crisis Prayer

Forty Days of Care and Prayer for the Caregiver

Dr. Dan R. Crawford
Dr. Vicki L. Gilliam

Copyright © 2020, Dan R. Crawford and Vicki L. Gilliam
All rights reserved. No part of this publication may be reproduced or transmitted in any form or by any means, electronic or mechanical, including photocopying and recording, or by any information storage and retrieval system, except in the case of brief quotations for use in articles and reviews, without written permission from the author.
The views expressed in the book are the author's and do not necessarily reflect those of the publisher.

Portions of this book were published earlier as a part of Vicki L. Gilliam's book, *Forty Days of Care for the Caregiver*, published by Pleasant Word, a division of WinePress Publishing, Enumclaw, WA, 2004, and are used here by permission.

Unless otherwise noted, all Scriptures are taken from the Holy Bible, New International Version, Copyright © 1973, 1978, 1984 by the International Bible Society. Used by permission of Zondervan Publishing House. The "NIV" and "New International Version" trademarks are registered in the United States Patent and Trademark Office by International Bible Society. Scripture references marked KJV are taken from the King James Version of the Bible. Scripture quotations marked HCSB have been taken from the Holman Christian Standard Bible, Copyright © 1999, 2000, 2001, 2002 by Holman Bible Publishers. Used by permission. Scripture quotations marked GWT are taken from the God's Word Translation, Copyright © 1995 by World Publishing, Inc. Used by permission.

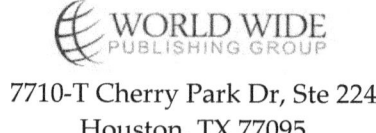

7710-T Cherry Park Dr, Ste 224
Houston, TX 77095

ISBN: 978-1-0879-1108-3

Vicki L. Gilliam

This book is dedicated to my mother, Lucille Mabry Gilliam, who was both caregiver and care recipient in my life, caring for me in innumerable ways.

Dan R. Crawford

This book is also dedicated to our grandparents, Alvis L. and Ethel Gilliam, who cared for us during the early years of our lives, then allowed us to care for them in the later years of their lives.

ENDORSEMENTS

I cannot express the perfect timing of this book. As my husband Benny and I care for my almost 97-year-old father, I have needed every day's Crisis Care encouragement, advice, Scriptures, and prayers. I have especially appreciated them because of my own immune-compromising illnesses that make caring more difficult. What particularly spoke to me came from Vicki's Days 17 and 23 about saying, "No," to set boundaries and from "Recharging Your Batteries." As we face decisions about Dad's care, I have found Dan's thoughts on "Nevertheless" the Lord's will be done from "The Role of Prayer in a Time of Crisis" to be a special reminder. The Crisis Prayer on Day Twenty-Nine from 1 John 4:18 concerning "no fear in love" has helped with our decision for my father.

Dr. Sharon Gresham: Founder/Director, *Ashes to Crowns Ministries*, Burleson, Texas; Resident Fellow and Coordinator of the *Carroll Prayer Network* (CPN) at *B.H. Carroll Theological Institute*, Irving, Texas.

From the first paragraph of *Crisis Care Crisis Prayer: Forty Days of Care and Prayer for the Caregiver* Dr. Gilliam and Dr. Crawford have captured the essence of the caregiver's needs. I am acquainted with the authors and their lifetime commitment to serving the needs of others. For thirteen years I watched as my wonderful wife, Dixie, disappeared behind dementia's devastating cloud. Each day took her farther away. For more than eleven years I was her caregiver, but she spent her last fifteen months in a memory care facility. Dixie died in July, 2018. During Dixie's journey I read exhaustively about dementia, terminal illness and care giving but nothing prepared me for the demands of long-term care giving, and nothing spoke to my spiritual needs like this wonderful text would have. I encourage caregivers and future caregivers to give God the opportunity to speak to you of His presence through this organized and spiritually prepared book.

Carroll D. Duke: Chief of Police, Retired, Gatesville, Texas.

Contents

Foreword 1

Why a Book for Caregivers? 3

The Role of Prayer in a Time of Crisis 8

DAY ONE: Trusting Christ in Crisis 14

DAY TWO: Taking Care of You 17

DAY THREE: Wrapping in the Warmth 20

DAY FOUR: Being Content 23

DAY FIVE: Showing Our Love 26

DAY SIX: Giving and Receiving 29

DAY SEVEN: Resting and Sleeping 32

DAY EIGHT: Finding Companionship 34

DAY NINE: Overcoming Anger 37

DAY TEN: Having Patience 40

DAY ELEVEN: Maintaining Dignity 43

DAY TWELVE: Finding Laughter 46

DAY THIRTEEN: Accepting Change 49

DAY FOURTEEN: Holding On through the Rough Times 51

DAY FIFTEEN: Being Satisfied, Not "Sandwiched" 53

DAY SIXTEEN: Putting On The Armor 56

DAY SEVENTEEN: Saying "No" 59

DAY EIGHTEEN: Finding Beauty 62

DAY NINETEEN: Putting the Pieces Together 65

DAY TWENTY: Encouraging Independence 68

DAY TWENTY-ONE: Evaluating Yourself...................................71
DAY TWENTY-TWO: Using Words Constructively................74
DAY TWENTY-THREE: Recharging Your Batteries 77
DAY TWENTY-FOUR: Working Together for Good 80
DAY TWENTY-FIVE: Staying Put..83
DAY TWENTY-SIX: Walking Toward the Light.......................86
DAY TWENTY-SEVEN: Carrying On 89
DAY TWENTY-EIGHT: Working Behind the Scenes..............92
DAY TWENTY-NINE: Caring in Sickness and in Health.......95
DAY THIRTY: Getting it Right 98
DAY THIRTY-ONE: Controling Worry and Anxiety............101
DAY THIRTY-TWO: Caring for the Terminally Ill.................104
DAY THIRTY-THREE: Learning Lessons from a Cat 107
DAY THIRTY-FOUR: Relating to Others 110
DAY THIRTY-FIVE: Moving Beyond Good Intentions 113
DAY THIRTY-SIX: Looking Up 116
DAY THIRTY-SEVEN: Overcoming Obstacles 119
DAY THIRTY-EIGHT: Improving as a Caregiver...................122
DAY THIRTY-NINE: Saying Goodbye......................................125
DAY FORTY: Saying Hello Again...127
APPENDIX A: Caregiver's Self-Rating Scale...........................130
End Notes..132

FOREWORD

First cousins, Dr. Dan Crawford and Dr. Vicki Gilliam, team up to write a healthy guide for caregivers, with Vicki writing the daily content, sub-titled CRISIS CARE, and Dan following up with the CRISIS PRAYER.

After agreeing to team up in this timely and unique fashion, they further agreed to add an additional point of uniqueness by inviting me to "Step Foreword" and make it a "tag team match," since I am uniquely Vicki's only sibling and Dan's only other cousin on this side of his family!

To top it off, we all three genetically share the same set of grandparents, Alvis and Ethel Gilliam, to whom this unique publication is co-dedicated!

This puts me in the unique position to brag knowledgeably on Dan's and Vicki's outstanding collaboration and prepare the reader for an immeasurable blessing, somewhat comparable to the deep, succulent satisfaction that lingers following your most memorable Thanksgiving meal!

A wise man once said, "If you would be pungent, be brief – for words, like sunbeams, pierce deepest when concentrated!" In keeping with such anticipation, therefore, I conclude this Foreword – and declare you to be "released for the feast," as you consume and be consumed by the healthy, tasty truth to be digested herein by your spirit, soul, and body!

Amen!

Dr. Larry Gilliam, Executive Director, *Gilliam Counseling & Development, Inc. Dayspring Counseling Services; Dayspring Institute for Training & Development*

WHY A BOOK FOR CAREGIVERS?

Vicki L. Gilliam

"When one is sick… two need help."
The Well Spouse Foundation

Why write a devotional book of "care and prayer" specifically for the caregiver? Consider these recent statistics reported by the National Family Caregivers Association:

- More than 65 million people, 29% of the U.S. population, provide care for a chronically ill, disabled, or aged family member or friend during any given year, and spend an average of 20 hours per week providing care for their loved one.

- Caregiving is no longer predominantly a women's issue. Men now make up approximately one-third of the caregiving population.

- As of the 2010 census, the fastest growing segment of the U.S. population is people aged 80 years and older, with a growth rate twice that for those 65 years and older, and almost four times that for the total population. Today, this group comprises 10% of the older population but is expected to more than triple in the next 40 years.

- Between 40% to 70% of family caregivers have clinically significant symptoms of depression with approximately one-quarter to half of these caregivers meeting the diagnostic criteria for major depression.

- Heavy duty caregivers, especially spousal caregivers, do not get consistent help from other family members. One study has shown that as many as three-fourths of these caregivers are "going it alone."

- Approximately 78% of adults living in the community and in need of long-term care depend on family and friends as their only source of help.

- According to a 2006 study by Met Life, American businesses can lose as much as $34 billion each year due to employees' need to care for loved ones 50 years of age and older.

- The value of the services family caregivers provide "for free," when caring for older adults, is estimated to be $375 billion a year. That is almost twice as much as is spent on homecare and nursing home services combined ($158 billion).

- More than half of the adult population either is or expects to be a family caregiver.[1]

In the so-called "graying of America," the median age of the United States population has been rising and is expected to continue to rise well into the mid-twenty-first century. In 1900, one American in twenty-five was age sixty-five or older; in 1984, one in nine. By 2050, it is estimated that one in five Americans will be sixty-five or older, as the "baby-boom" generation continues to age.[2]

Senior adults are not the only population that requires caregiving, however. Advances in medicine and medical technology result in people with significant physical and cognitive needs living longer and in greater numbers. More and more, family members are called upon to become caregivers to adult siblings with cognitive challenges, loved ones with life-changing injuries, extremely premature babies, and children with significant disabilities. As of 2010, approximately 16.6% of

Americans (39.8 million caregivers) provide care to adults (aged 18+) with a disability.[3]

Another trend in current American society finds senior adults caring for relatives under the age of eighteen. In 2014, the Census Bureau reported that 6% of American households contained a co-resident grandparent and grandchild, while in 1970, that figure was 3%. Sixty percent of those households were headed by grandparents, which translated to 2.7 million grandparents caring for grandchildren, a 7% rise from 2009.[4]

Former First Lady Rosalynn Carter summarizes statistics such as these in a thought-provoking manner:

> *There are only four kinds of people in this world:*
> *Those who have been caregivers,*
> *Those who currently are caregivers,*
> *Those who will be caregivers, and*
> *Those who will need caregivers.*[5]

Obviously, the physical, emotional, and economic implications of these trends are significant. Organizations such as the American Association of Retired Persons (AARP), Caregiver Action Network, the National Alliance for Caregiving, the National Family Caregivers Association, the Family Caregiver Alliance, and other private and governmental agencies are reaching out to caregivers to address these needs. However, caregivers also have spiritual needs that may not be addressed so readily. The purpose of this book is to address these spiritual needs while providing helpful and inspirational information to the caregiver.

Who is a caregiver? My favorite definition is from the National Family Caregiver Association: "We are family, friends, and neighbors who stand by those we love as they face chronic illness or disability. We share a common bond with each other despite the fact that some of us care for our spouses, while others care for parents, children or [other loved ones], and despite the fact that we deal with a wide array of medical conditions and diagnoses."[6]

For the purpose of this book, the definition can be expanded to include those who provide care for a living. "Professional" caregivers such as nurses, home health care providers, and nursing home or hospice staff may also find inspiration from these pages.

Why "forty days" of care? Obviously, forty days do not translate into a week, a month, or any other common grouping of days; however, Bible students have long considered forty days to be spiritually significant. Remember, Noah was in the flood for 40 days and 40 nights; Moses was on Mount Sinai for 40 days and 40 nights; and Jesus was in the wilderness for 40 days and 40 nights -- to name a few. In the numeric system of the Scriptures, the number "40" consistently is associated with completion and with spiritual preparation.[7]

It is my hope that as you complete these forty days of care and prayer, you will be more spiritually prepared to realize the joys and to deal with the challenges that come from caregiving.

Why me? A caregiver myself, I decided to write a devotional book for caregivers after retiring with more than thirty years in education. Most of those years were spent working in special education programs for students with disabilities and their parents. Professionally, I have experienced first-hand the care and dedication given by parents, loved ones, and teachers to children and teenagers with significant disabilities.

In addition to working with individuals with special needs, I have felt God's call to three other specific things in my life: (1) children's ministries when I was younger, (2) senior adult ministries when I couldn't keep up with the kids anymore, and (3) caring for my mother when advancing age and medical conditions created that need. These areas of my life have given me professional and personal experiences that I have incorporated into these devotionals and that, hopefully, will provide inspiration for others to whom God has entrusted the care of a loved one.

In this book, you will find forty daily devotionals, related Scripture passages, and Scripture-modeled prayers for the crises that are sure to occur while caregiving. Integrated into these devotionals are facts and tips for caregivers from numerous national and state caregiver resources so that they will be informational as well as inspirational. My prayer is that, as you study these pages, you will find or renew the faith, hope, and love so necessary in the life and heart of a very special person – a caregiver.

> *"You are quiet heroes, unknown except to your loved one and closest friends."*
> **Nancy Wexler**, *gerontologist*

THE ROLE OF PRAYER IN A TIME OF CRISIS

Dan R. Crawford

For more than two decades I occupied the Chair of Prayer at Southwestern Baptist Theological Seminary, and I was often asked in crisis times why and what believers pray in times of crisis. Columbine High School. Texas A&M University Bonfire. Murrah Federal Building in Oklahoma City. 9/11. Every time the question came, the question I asked myself was about Jesus praying in a crisis? What would Jesus do?

Then came the crises of the viruses. I remember landing in the Vancouver, Canada airport and entering the Customs area only to realize that we had landed just a few minutes after the Jumbo Jet from Hong Kong. Standing ahead of me in the Customs line were hundreds of Chinese, all wearing face masks. Then there was Ebola crisis where Doctors and Nurses contracted the virus from attending their patients and churches learned to use the virtual hug during their welcome time. Then came the Coronavirus/COVID-19, a global pandemic so vicious and fast moving that to quote stats would only be sharing numbers that were incorrect and irrelevant within hours. What would Jesus do?

Then there are the personal and family crises – never covered in the news; never picked up by media, but nonetheless painful and devastating to those whom it touches. Specifically, I wondered about the caregiver in the crisis. What would be the role of prayer for the caregiver? What would Jesus do?

As a matter of fact, Jesus had a few crises. What did He do? He faced the biggest crisis of His life in a prayer garden - The

Garden of Gethsemane. His actions on that night are recorded in Matthew 26:38-42:

> *Then He said to them, "My soul is exceedingly sorrowful, even to death. Stay here and watch with Me. "He went a little farther and fell on His face, and prayed, saying, "O My Father, if it is possible, let this cup pass from Me; nevertheless, not as I will, but as You will."*
>
> *Then He came to the disciples and found them sleeping, and said to Peter, "What! Could you not watch with Me? The spirit indeed is willing, but the flesh is weak." Again, a second time, He went away and prayed, saying, "O My Father, if this cup cannot pass away from Me unless drink it, Your will be done*[1]

This account in the life of Jesus is also recorded in Luke 22:43, and there we find the end of the story: *"Then an angel appeared to Him from heaven, strengthening Him."*

So, before we begin to look at *Crisis Care Crisis Prayer: Forty Days of Care and Prayer for the Caregiver*, let's consider what Jesus did in similar times. Crisis praying is different from other kinds of prayer. Crisis praying is by nature a spasmodic cry of emergency rather than the consistent communication of a godly life. Crisis is not the best time to get acquainted or re-acquainted with God. In fact, he prays best in crisis, who prays consistently before crisis. So, how do we pray in times of crisis?

Consider the model of Jesus, praying in the crisis of Gethsemane. A few minutes before the Gethsemane experience, Jesus had been in an upper room in Jerusalem, observing the Passover meal with His disciples. Judas, who had been identified as the one who would betray Jesus, had departed the room. When Jesus added that another of the disciples would deny knowing Him, Peter had vigorously denied that it would be he. Roman soldiers would soon be looking for Jesus. In the semi-privacy of Gethsemane, Jesus prayed.

Facing imminent death Jesus faced the crisis head-on – *"Stay here and watch with Me"* . . . *"He went a little farther and fell on His face and prayed"* (Matthew 26:39). Sometimes it seems God is silent when we want Him to respond to us. However, it is often the case, that as we pray, God responds. In the midst of that Gethsemane prayer time, Jesus defined the crisis – *"My soul is exceedingly sorrowful, even to death"* (Matthew 26:38). Contrary to Jesus, we sometimes want to face away from the crisis, deny it, ignore it, refuse to believe it. But a crisis will never be properly cared for, until we face it.

Jesus called on His Father. *"O My Father"* (Matthew 26:39). Only children of God can be assured of being heard when they call on their heavenly father. While others may be heard, there is sufficient biblical evidence that God listens to the prayers of His children. To send the prayer anywhere else is useless, although I read often of someone who is "sending prayers your way." If I find myself in a crisis, please do not send your prayers my way. I can do nothing with them. God can. Address your prayers FOR me, but TO God.

Jesus evaluated the options – *"If it is possible, let this cup pass from Me"* (Matthew 26:39). I found one, rather theologically liberal commentary that said the *"cup"* was not a reference to the cross. Every other reference I checked, agreed that the *"cup"* was a reference to the cross. How could Jesus pray this? He was simply following scripture.

The Psalmist said, *"Delight yourself also in the Lord, and He shall give you the desires of your heart"* (Psalm 37:4). In other words, share with God the desires of your heart. The writer of Hebrews wrote, *"Let us therefore come boldly to the throne of grace, that we may obtain mercy and find grace to help in time of need"* (Hebrews 4:16).

Of course, if it were any other kind of throne, we likely could not approach it, but it is a throne of *"grace"* therefore, we approach *"boldly,"* with the desires of our heart. Jesus knew what the *"cup"* meant, but He also knew of *"certain Greeks"* who had arrived in Jerusalem *"to worship at the feast"* (John 12:20). Could these not be the *"other sheep"* (John 10:16) that God had promised would respond to the Gospel? Would it not be better than death, for Jesus to go back home with these *"Greeks"* to begin a whole new ministry there? So, Jesus evaluated His options and went to the Father with His requests. In the midst of our crises, as we evaluate the options, we have every reason to beseech God to, "Stop the crisis!"

Jesus prayed the one word that must be included in every prayer request – *"Nevertheless"* (Matthew 26:39). This word allows for God's greater will to be done. A father or mother makes a decision for the good of the family. One or more family members don't like it, or don't agree with it. However, because the decision is for the good of the overall family, they respond favorably.

This one word and one verse got me through my teen-age years. At the age of fifteen, I was involved in a terrible automobile accident. A driver with a much-too-high alcohol content, hit our vehicle, spun us around, throwing me out of the vehicle, and causing the fracture of the second vertebrae of my neck. Because a break in this vertebra usually results in death or paralysis, and because I was not either dead or paralyzed, I became a sort of medical experiment. I spent nine months of my High School Sophomore year, sleeping in a hospital bed, with a homebound teacher, away from my friends. Twice I was scheduled for surgery that would have wired the bones of my neck together, making it immobile. Both were cancelled almost at the last minute. Once I had even been prepped for surgery.

But my father was a rather popular pastor in Houston, Texas, and my mother was President of the Pastors' Wives Fellowship. These two groups, plus other friends, interceded to God on my behalf, and prayed me through. I made it back to High School in time to participate in athletics for my senior year, and even enrolled in college on a partial baseball scholarship. The verse that helped get me through this crisis was Romans 8:28, *"We know that all things work together for good to those who love God, to those who are the called according to His purpose"* It is the verse that can get caregivers through any crisis. It does not say that all things are good. They are not. It affirms that *"all things,"* even things that we would describe as crisis, *"work together for good."* Somehow, beyond our understanding, God chooses to work in all things, even crisis things, to bring about *"good"* for His forever family.

In the midst of my personal teen-age crisis, with all my human *"desires"* and with all *"boldness,"* I came to a firm decision – in spite of the nature of my crisis, I prayed *"nevertheless"* which meant – whatever, wherever, whenever, why ever, however? – I belonged to God. He had responded to my cries and the intercession of my friends, and He had spared my life and allowed me to be whole. Now, I belonged to Him. A complete understanding and yielding to this one word – *"nevertheless"* – allows us to accept whatever details of the crisis affect us.

Jesus came to a firm decision – *"Your will be done"* (Matthew 26:42). Part of every Scripture-modeled prayer is yielding to His will. Several years ago, my wife fell and fractured her pelvis. This was followed by trauma surgery and the announcement that she would be immobile for six months. I cleared my calendar to become her primary caregiver. My lifestyle changed – physically, emotionally, spiritually. Shortly after the six months, it was determined that she needed a complete hip replacement. Once again, I became the primary caregiver. This was God's will for me. I prayed with my desires, even boldly so. Then I prayed "nevertheless" and I yielded to God's will for me. Crisis may change many things, alter much of lifestyle, but it must not remove us from God's will.

Outside of God's will there is fear. Psalm 23:4 affirms, "Yea, though I walk through the valley of the shadow of death, I will fear no evil, for You are with me." Most crises are "evil" and cause us to be fearful. Some even lead toward *"death"* or at least the *"shadow of death."* However, when you pray correctly in crisis, and come to a firm decision, that His will can be done, and you will accept it, you need not fear. So, *"walk,"* don't run, relax, don't panic, through your crisis.

So, what's in it for me? This is often a "bottom-line" question for this generation. In Luke's account of the Gethsemane experience, another dimension of crisis praying appears, namely that Jesus was empowered to face the crisis – *"Then an angel appeared to Him from heaven, strengthening Him"* (Luke 22:43). We say, we're not sure we have the strength to survive the crisis. Perhaps it is because of economic issues, or relational challenges, or family circumstances. We feel we lack the strength with which to cope, much less, survive. Don't forget angels. These are God's messengers, whom the writer of Hebrews describes as *"ministering spirits sent forth to minister for those who will inherit salvation"* (Hebrews 1:14). So, whether it is angels, the Holy Spirit, whom Jesus described as, *"another Helper . . .who will abide with you forever,"* (John 14:16) or the very presence of God Himself, there is strength available to help the believer, the caregiver, in the midst of any and every crisis.

Crisis times will come. Caregiving will be needed. Prayer will be essential. Correct, Scripture-modeled prayer will be more effective.

DAY ONE: TRUSTING CHRIST IN CRISIS

CRISIS CARE: Caregiving frequently begins with a crisis — an unwelcomed diagnosis, a life-altering injury, a grim prognosis, or even the death of a previous caregiver. "A life-changing moment can happen in the blink of an eye. Most caregivers did not plan for this journey. Truthfully, most were just thrown unsuspectingly into it." As a result, it's easy for caregivers to stay in crisis and live each day wondering. "What is going to happen next?"[1]

As caregiver Frank Joseph said in a United Way impact statement, "There is no way to understand the depth of caregiving unless you are in it. And then it becomes totally consuming and isolating."[2]

Suddenly becoming a caregiver can have a major impact on almost every area of your life, resulting in feelings of devastation and being overwhelmed. As with other crises, the crisis of caregiving can also trigger what grief expert David Kessler calls "anticipatory grief," that feeling we get about what the future holds when we are uncertain. Anticipatory grief, he says, is the mind going to the future and imagining the worst.[3]

And so, when faced with the crises of caregiving, how should Christian caregivers respond? Here are five Biblical principles offered by Rick Warren when facing a crisis:

(1) Release your grief. "It does no good to stuff emotions or deny they exist. God created us to feel emotions, and he doesn't expect us to act happy when we're grieving."

(2) Be willing to receive help from others. "It's a huge mistake to isolate yourself when you're going through a crisis.

We all need the support, encouragement, and presence of other people, particularly in the aftermath of tragedy."

(3) Choose not to be bitter. "We all have the power to decide how tragedy affects us.... One skill that will help people make the choice to be happy is learning to focus on what's left—not what's lost."

(4) Remember what in your life is of real value. "A crisis helps us clarify our values by showing us what really matters and what really doesn't matter.... Don't confuse your possessions with your purpose in life."

(5) Recognize that this is the time to rely on Christ. "A crisis creates a moment in your life when you can shift your dependence to something that can never be taken from you.... He promised to never leave us or forsake us—and that's an eternal security we can build our lives on."[4]

CRISIS PRAYER: "So do not fear, for I am with you; do not be dismayed, for I am your God. I will strengthen you and help you; I will uphold you with my righteous right hand." (Isaiah 41:10)

When God promises to be *"with"* us the word used means *"equally with."* He is not just alongside of us, or nearby us. He is *"equally with"* us. To not *"fear"* or to not be *"dismayed"* means not to be bewildered, but rather to trust in God. We are to trust God because He will *"strengthen"* us meaning, He will make us stout, strong, bold, alert, and He will *"help"* us. Furthermore, God will *"uphold"* us meaning, He will sustain, keep fast. The two verbs, *"strengthen"* and *"uphold"* are in the past tense. While primarily they declare past favors, they may also be regarded as prophetic of future ones, since God, *"does not change like shifting shadows"* (James 1:17).

1. Dear Lord, thank You for being ever-present with me to offer strength amid crisis. Thanks for *"upholding"* me and for holding me up. You have done this with Your people in the past, and I anticipate You doing it with me today, as I:

2. In addition, Lord, I'd like to share the following with You:

All at once my whole world changed;
Life itself was rearranged.
Help me know He paid the price.
Crisis comes, but so does Christ.

DAY TWO: TAKING CARE OF YOU

CRISIS CARE: Caregivers need care, too! We all know it, but we just have a hard time doing it. A recent study by the National Alliance for Caregiving and the AARP found that more than half of those who provide major care for a loved one experience stress and emotional strain. AARP considers this finding a major concern since prolonged stress can lead to significant emotional and physical consequences. As a result, taking care of ourselves is one of the most important aspects of taking care of others effectively.

"Because you're responsible for the welfare of another person, taking care of yourself is doubly important," says the American Heart Association. "You need to stay rested, refreshed and energetic both for yourself and for the person you care for."[1]

PacifiCare offers similar advice: "You, the caregiver, are incredibly important. The welfare of another person depends upon you. If you are not in good health, that other person may also suffer. So, if you've taken on the role of a caregiver, you've also accepted a special responsibility to take care of yourself. That means taking care of yourself physically, emotionally, mentally, spiritually, interpersonally, and financially."[2]

What are some practical ways that we, as caregivers, can take care of ourselves? AARP offers these suggestions: (1) take care of your health, especially nutrition, exercise, and sleep, (2) maintain or establish social contacts to avoid isolation, (3) ask friends and relatives for help with daily tasks and errands, (4) deal constructively with negative feelings, and (5) find time for yourself to unwind and to have fun. Also, avoid bottled-up feelings by talking with family and friends about the rewards and challenges of caregiving and by sharing your experiences with coworkers in similar situations.[3]

Taking care of ourselves physically and emotionally is key, but even more importantly, we must take care of ourselves spiritually. Finding time for prayer, Bible study, worship, and Christian fellowship is vital in the spiritual life of a caregiver. All of these things take time, but they give us the strength to do more with the time that remains. And remember, God's Word gives us a precious promise: God cares for each of us, and because He cares, He desires that we give our frustrations, our concerns, and our cares to Him. Lean on Him. He is the very best Caregiver!

CRISIS PRAYER: *"Cast all your cares on Him because He cares for you."* (1 Peter 5:7).

This is a quotation from Psalm 55:22, *"Cast your cares on the Lord and he will sustain you; he will never let the righteous be shaken."* The Greek word *epi* translated "cast" means to throw and when you add the Greek word, *rhipto* it means to throw upon. In other words, we are not to simply throw or cast away our cares, but we are to cast or throw them upon the Lord, and furthermore, we are not simply to cast or throw some of our cares, but *"all"* of them. What are we throwing or casting? We're throwing or casting *"cares"* and the word is also translated anxieties or worries. Why are we instructed to throw or cast all of these cares on the Lord? *"Because He cares for you."* The first *"care"* mentioned in this verse relates to worldly things which trouble us and distract our minds. The second *"care,"* God's *"care,"* is a different Greek word, meaning concern or thoughtful interest. So, as caregivers, what should we pray?

1. Dear Lord, thank You that I do not have to bear my own burdens, and carry my concerns, but can transfer all of them to You. Thank You that You not only are willing to accept them, but You are able to bear them. Specifically, today, I need to cast upon You the following care:

2. In addition, Lord, I'd like to share the following with You:

Help us turn to You, dear Lord,
When things are tough, and times are hard
And every time we shed a tear,
Help us remember you are near.

DAY THREE: WRAPPING IN THE WARMTH

CRISIS CARE: Like most of you, I am a caregiver. I had the privilege and the challenge of caring for my mother, who lived with me about thirteen years until her death at age 93. By the time she reached her mid-eighties, my mother had lost her ability to bathe and dress alone due to a series of strokes that affected her motor skills more than her communication or memory. When I first began helping with her bath and drying her afterwards, she seemed to enjoy the baths and appreciate the help, but she was always cold, especially when she first got out of the tub. We tried warmer water, faster baths, and extra heaters, but nothing seemed to get rid of that initial chill.

Then one day, I had an idea. Before her bath, I placed her towel in the clothes dryer to warm, and as she exited the bathtub, I wrapped the warm towel all the way around her upper body in a bear-hug fashion. The warm towel dispelled the chill, and the "bear hug" technique basically dried her entire upper body all at once. "Oh, that feels so good it makes me want to purr," she exclaimed, and warm towels quickly became a regular part of our bath routine. Especially on cold mornings, wrapping in the warmth of a heated towel protected her from the cold surroundings. (And I don't think she minds the big hug either!)

We are much the same in our spiritual lives. We can grow cold spiritually when the demands of life steal our time to be quiet and still before God. We can feel cold and alone when we are moving too fast to feel the warmth of the Son. We may even find ourselves crying out as David did, *"Therefore is my spirit overwhelmed within me; my heart within me is desolate"* (Psalm 143:4 KJV).

When the world seems cold and desolate all around you, and when the remedies of this world don't seem to help, allow God to wrap you in the warmth of His love and hold you in the strength of His arms.

CRISIS PRAYER: *"How precious is Your lovingkindness, O God! Therefore the children of men put their trust under the shadow of Your wings."* (Psalm 36:7 HCSB)

The Greek word for *precious*, means rare, or splendid. God's *"lovingkindness"* is not only *"precious"* but it is also rare and splendid.

In verse 5, the Palmist made mention of the *"loving-kindness of God"* as His most characteristic quality. Now he brings it into notice as God's provision for all His creatures. It is his *"lovingkindness"* or his *"kindness."* that allows *"the children of men"* to *"put their trust"* or *"take refuge"* or *"flee for protection, "under the shadow"* of God's wings, a phrase that the Psalmist uses multiple times (Psalm 17:8; Psalm 57:1; Psalm 63:7, etc.), and refers to God's protection for our safety.

1. Dear Lord, thank You for loving me enough to offer Your protection, and for allowing me to offer Your protection to those whom I serve. Wrapped in Your wings, I find security and comfort, and then am able to pass it on. As I care for others today, I ask You for the following care:

2. In addition, Lord, I'd like to share the following with You:

Thank you for the love you give
Every moment that we live.
You will keep us safe and warm
In your strong and loving arms.

DAY FOUR: BEING CONTENT

CRISIS CARE: Caregivers often completely change their lifestyles to take care of those they love.[1] For some Christians, this lifestyle change may involve their public service to the Lord. Consider the following poem by Ruth Harms Calkin:

"I Wonder"

You know, Lord, how I serve You

With great emotional fervor

In the limelight.

You know how eagerly I speak for You

At the women's club.

You know how I effervesce when I promote

A fellowship group.

You know my genuine enthusiasm

At a Bible study.

But how would I react, I wonder,

If You pointed to a basin of water

And asked me to wash the calloused feet

Of a bent and wrinkled old woman

Day after day

Month after month

In a room where nobody saw

And nobody knew.[2]

These words may become an accurate "before-and-after" portrait for Christians who become caregivers. The "what if" of the second verse becomes reality, and years of very public service are replaced with the very private calling of caring for a loved one. With such a change in lifestyle, how do caregivers stay content? In Philippians 4:12, Paul says he has learned the secret of being content in any and every situation. What is Paul's secret of contentment? His answer can be found in the next verse: "I can do **all** things through Christ who strengthens me" [HCSB, EMPHASIS ADDED]. When we seek His purpose in every stage of our lives, Christ will give us strength to do whatever He calls us to do, whether it be in the spotlight or in a room where nobody sees, and nobody knows.

CRISIS PRAYER: *". . . for I have learned to be content whatever the circumstances. I know what it is to be in need, and I know what it is to have plenty. I have learned the secret of being content in any and every situation . . ."* (Philippians 4:11b–12a)

What has Paul learned? The word, "I" is emphatic, meaning he does not assume everyone else, or anyone else has learned this, but he has learned to *"be content,"* that is, to be self-sufficient, contented, satisfied regardless of his *"circumstances,"* though it involves all the hardships of captivity. The word *"content"* was an oft-used Stoic word, but Paul borrows it to speak of his Christian experience, an experience that has taught him how to be in need, that is to fall short, as well as how to act when he has *"plenty,"* that is, when he excels. Paul applies this experiential knowledge to *"any and all situations"* or we might say, to each and every one.

1. Dear Lord, thank You for the knowledge gained from You that makes me *"content"* in every *"situation."* I confess that my *"situation"* is difficult and that I cannot handle it alone. So, as I care for others today, I ask You for the following:

2. In addition, Lord, I'd like to share the following with You:

> *Lord, I can serve you on a stage*
> *Or in a room or on a page.*
> *Help me love "the least of these,"*
> *Especially when no one sees.*

DAY FIVE: SHOWING OUR LOVE

CRISIS CARE: I do a lot of online shopping for Christmas and birthday gifts, and as a result, I receive a multitude of catalogs. One in today's mail advertised a caregiver coffee mug. On the mug was this reminder: "Take good care every day to show your love in a special way."[1]

How can a caregiver show her love every day in a special way? To be sure, all the routine tasks of caregiving should demonstrate the caregiver's love, but how can we go above and beyond the routine to show love in a special way? Of course, there are tangible things such as cards, flowers, gifts, and such, but sometimes the most important things cost little or no money. Here are a few suggestions:

- Listen to your loved one. Finding time to listen to stories and memories—even if you've heard them more than once—affirms that what he has to say is important.

- Take time with your loved one to enjoy something she enjoys. Too often, I found myself starting a video for my mother and then moving on to do something else, when I know she enjoyed the movie more when I watched it with her.

- Don't underestimate the soothing effect of music and the pleasant memories it can bring to mind. Researchers tell us that hearing and responding to music is one of the last things to be lost to aging, injury, or disability. Learn about your loved one's favorite songs and favorite singers, and then find ways for him to hear them.[2]

- Remember that we never outgrow the need for human touch. If you're not a hugger, a gentle squeeze on the shoulder or even applying lotion or aftershave provides a loving touch that not only communicates your affection but also produces a heightened sense of well-being and security. Scientists tell us that appropriate touch even prompts the brain to produce endorphins, the body's natural pain suppressors, leading to a decreased perception of pain. [3]
- And perhaps most importantly, don't let what you are doing become more important than the who you are doing it for. For example, a home-cooked meal is wonderful, but sometimes buying or fixing something simple so that you will have time to sit and visit with a loved one may be more important and meaningful for both of you.[4]

Take good care every day to show your love in a special way. That was a reminder I needed today. It's interesting how the Lord can speak even through a mail-order catalog!

CRISIS PRAYER: *"Dear friends, let us love one another, for love comes from God. Everyone who loves has been born of God and knows God." (1 John 4:7)*

John is asking his readers to *"love"* with *agape,* or God's kind of love. The word means, to take pleasure in, to long for. Not only have we been *"born of God,"* we also *"know"* God. This is the obvious product of the true knowledge of God, because God is love (1 John 4:7-8). The absence of love is ignorance of God, since real knowledge of God shows His nature. If we are asked how we know of God's love, the answer is that it is seen in His Son, Jesus. In sending Jesus, God loved us without any love on our part. Our relation to God reminds us that we must have the same love to each other.

1. Dear Lord, thank You for allowing me to know you and for creating me with the ability to love others with Your of kind of love. Related to loving others, I ask You for:

2. In addition, Lord, I'd like to share the following with You:

Help me listen and really hear
And know the things that they hold dear,
So things I do are never more
Important than those I do them for.

DAY SIX: GIVING AND RECEIVING

CRISIS CARE: In June 2002, I was diagnosed with breast cancer. Thankfully, it was very early stage and could be handled with a partial mastectomy and radiation treatments. Surgery was in July, and I was back at work in three days. I assumed the worst was over . . . and then the radiation treatments began.

Every day, for seven weeks, Monday through Friday, I drove to the cancer center first thing in the morning for my treatments, and then went straight to work. By the end of the third week, the radiation had begun to take its toll, and at the end of each workday, I was just drained. As my friends and family became aware, they began to find ways to help. My secretaries found ways to screen calls and keep my work schedule lighter than usual. My best friends took up the slack in caring for my mother. My staff members even worked out a schedule to provide our evening meal three days a week for a couple of months. In other words, for a period of time, I became the "care-receiver" rather than the "care-giver." It was wonderful—except for one thing: I tend to be more comfortable in the role of the giver than the taker. Although I knew I couldn't have made it without the help, I often felt awkward and uncomfortable accepting it.

Thinking back on that time in my life, I am reminded of Simon Peter. He also had a hard time receiving, especially from Jesus. Consider this case in point: To demonstrate the concept of servanthood, Jesus began to wash the disciples' feet. Peter objected, feeling unworthy to accept what was usually a servant's task from the Lord. Jesus made it very clear that on this particular occasion, He wanted Peter to be on the receiving end.

From childhood, most of us have learned "it is more blessed to give than to receive," and it is! However, there are times in our lives when the Lord intends for us to be on the receiving end, and He brings loving, compassionate people into our lives for that purpose. When we fail to accept their assistance, both we and they miss out on a wonderful blessing! In the words of Maya Angelou, "When we give cheerfully and accept gratefully, everyone is blessed."[1]

CRISIS PRAYER: *"'No,' said Peter, 'you shall never wash my feet.' Jesus answered, 'Unless I wash you, you have no part with me. 'Then Lord,' Peter replied, 'not just my feet but my hands and my head as well!'"* (John 13:8–9)

Peter was emphatic as evidenced by the word, "*never.*" Not only was Jesus not to wash Peter's feet, but He was "*never*" to do so. Once Jesus explained the consequences to Peter – "*You have no part with me,*" -- Peter quickly adjusted his feelings. That phrase is a Hebrew thought in Greek dress - frequently used in the Old Testament (see Deuteronomy 12:12). By the act of washing their feet, Jesus, their Lord, taught the disciples self-sacrifice and love in contrast to self-seeking and pride. This is a lesson every servant of Jesus must learn, for the servant is not greater than the Lord. The lesson is a hard one, but it is necessary one -- the strong must become as the little child before he can enter into the Kingdom of Heaven.

1. Dear Lord, thank You for demonstrating for me, through Peter, how to receive care. So, as I care for others today, I ask You for the following:

2. In addition, Lord, I'd like to share the following with You:

> *Lord, help me find a way to give*
> *To someone every day I live,*
> *But show me so that I believe.*
> *Sometimes You want me to receive.*

DAY SEVEN: RESTING AND SLEEPING

CRISIS CARE: Have you ever felt like the poet Robert Frost when he wrote, ". . . for I have promises to keep and miles to go before I sleep"? All of us experience days when we have more things to do than hours in the day to do them. We push ourselves long and hard, and then when we finally have a few hours to sleep, we can't or don't! Yet, as Dr. Dan Crawford reminds us in his book *DiscipleShape*, "Not even the greatest athlete can run all the time. Rest is as much a part of fitness as is activity.... Sometimes the most crucial thing you can do is sleep."[1]

The Alzheimer's Association identifies "sleeplessness" as one of ten warning signs of caregiver stress. When anxiety about facing another day or what the future holds, or a seemingly endless list of concerns robs the caregiver of sleep, exhaustion makes it nearly impossible to complete necessary daily tasks.[2]

Have you ever noticed how the Scriptures address every issue we encounter? Well, sleeplessness is no exception. The psalmist wrote, "Surely I will not enter my house, nor lie on my bed; I will not give sleep to my eyes or slumber to my eyelids, until I find a place for the Lord" (Psalm 132:3–5). As Dr. Crawford states, "Ignoring God at bedtime is a sure path to insomnia. On the other hand, reading God's word and communicating with God at bedtime beats sleeping pills."[3]

In Psalm 4, David also gives us this tip for a good night's sleep: ". . . when you are on your beds, search your hearts and be silent. Offer right sacrifices and trust in the Lord." The concerns of today and the anxieties about tomorrow come into proper perspective when we are quiet before the Lord and trust those things to the One who does not sleep or slumber. Knowing that truth, "when you lie down, you will not be afraid; when you lie down, your sleep will be sweet" (Proverbs 3:24).

CRISIS PRAYER: *"He will not let your foot slip—He who watches over you will not slumber; indeed, He who watches over Israel will neither slumber nor sleep."* (Psalm 121:3)

God will not allow your foot to *"slip."* The word also means to waver or fall, and is possible because, as some translations say, He is your *"protector,"* that is He is a hedge about you or a guard. He is a 24/7 God who does not *"slumber,"* meaning, to get drowsy, nor even sleep.

1. Dear Lord, thank You for always watching over me, even when I grow tired and sleepy. Would you please protect me today as I care for:

2. In addition, Lord, I'd like to share the following with You:

*Now I lay me down to sleep,
So, Lord, it's up to You to keep
My loved ones safe from harm and sorrow
Till we greet a new tomorrow.*

DAY EIGHT: FINDING COMPANIONSHIP

CRISIS CARE: Pookie the cat came to live with my mother a few months after my father died. Pookie was a stray who just took up residence, first on my mother's porch, then in her house, and then in her heart. They just seemed to adopt each other, which came as a surprise to me since my mom had never been especially interested in pets. I, on the other hand, had long been a "cat person" and was pleased to see the companionship and affection this newfound animal friend supplied. During the seven years my mother lived alone, Pookie provided many happy moments and quickly became the focus of my mother's home. I used to joke that she loved Pookie more than she loved me! Even after she and Pookie came to live with me, this feline family member filled the hours for her when she was home alone.

My mother was not alone in finding companionship with animal friends. "Pets are an important form of social contact," says Dr. Alan Beck, director of the Center for Human-Animal Bond at Purdue University.[1] "For older people who may be less mobile and who have few or limited companions, animals provide family and friendship, something to care for and to be recognized by." Studies also show that pets can improve physical health by reducing blood pressure, lowering stress, and aiding relaxation.[2]

Wasn't God thoughtful to give us the gift of pets? Each part of God's creation was made with a purpose, and when you think about it, one of the very first tasks God gave to Adam was to name the animals. God once again showed His care for animals when He instructed Noah to save not only humans, but animals of every kind. Even the new heaven and new earth promised after Christ's return is described with animals, where the "wolf also shall dwell with the lamb, and the leopard shall lie down with the kid . . . and a little child shall lead them" (Isaiah 11:6 KJV). As Cecil F. Alexander expressed so beautifully:

> All things bright and beautiful,
>
> All creatures great and small,
>
> All things wise and wonderful,
>
> The Lord God made them all.[3]

And that even includes dogs—a fact that's sometimes a little hard for us "cat people" to accept!

CRISIS PRAYER: *"Praise the Lord from the earth, you great sea creatures and all ocean depth . . . wild animals and all cattle, small creatures and flying birds….. Let everything that has breath, praise the Lord."* (Psalm 148:7, 10 & Psalm 150:6)

Psalm 148:1 has praise coming from *"the heavens"* and now it has worked its way down to where *"creatures "*of *"the earth"* join in, and eventually to the *"sea creatures"* in the *"ocean depth."* In other words, *"praise"* is everywhere, as the Psalmist concludes, *"Everything that has breath."* Thus, the Psalms end with a great expression of praise.

1. Dear Lord, while I thank you for what You have done, are doing, and will do, I praise you for who You are. You are praiseworthy. Remind me to praise You today as I:

2. In addition, Lord, I'd like to share the following with You:

For all these creatures great and small
We thank you, Lord; you made them all.
They show us devotion and loyalty
And love us unconditionally.

DAY NINE: OVERCOMING ANGER

CRISIS CARE: Even the most patient caregiver can find himself battling against anger, which may cause him to lash out at his loved one, which leads to feelings of guilt, which can make him feel angry again. Experts call it the anger-guilt-anger cycle, and it's quite common among caregivers.[1]

"Anger comes in many forms," writes Dee Dee Hunt for the International Scleroderma Network. "Anger that they are thrown into the position of caregiver. Anger at downward changes in their loved one's condition. Anger and frustration at the financial consequences experienced if there is a loss of income and health care costs. Anger at having feelings of anger. Anger that no one seems to notice how overwhelming the caregiver's job can be. Anger at loss of control over the situation."[2]

No matter how much the caregiver loves the care recipient, it's almost impossible never to become angry. What matters is what we do with that anger and how we handle it. Here are a few suggestions to get you through the eye of the storm: (1) Leave the room. Walking away, even for a minute or two, may keep you from doing or saying something you'll regret later. (2) Keep your perspective. Is the situation really worth getting angry about? (3) Laugh. Recognize and appreciate the humor in your day-to-day experiences. (4) Don't beat yourself up. If you slip into anger, find a constructive way to deal with it instead of taking a guilt trip. (5) Monitor the frequency and intensity of your anger. If anger permeates your life, you may need to consider a support group or counseling.[3]

Most importantly, follow Paul's advice in his letter to the Ephesians. Deal with anger sooner rather than later. When your anger spills over to your loved ones, don't let that day end without resolving the issue. Often that means putting aside our pride and saying, "I'm sorry." Even if you don't feel sorry for the entire incident right at that moment, you can always find at least one thing for which you can legitimately apologize, thus opening lines of communication. As the song lyrics say, "Love is something you do ... not always something you can feel."[4] It may also mean admitting we were wrong. These things are not easy to do, but they are vital to keep anger from mushrooming into bitterness, resentment, and unfortunately in some cases, abusive behaviors.

Paul states it very clearly in Ephesians 4: "Get rid of all bitterness, rage and anger, brawling and slander, along with every form of malice." Then he goes on to tell us how: "Be kind and compassionate to one another, forgiving each other, just as in Christ God forgave you. Be imitators of God, therefore . . . and live a life of love." If, as an act of obedience, we begin to do deeds of kindness, compassion, and love, our feelings will soon follow suit. In doing so, we are effectively controlling our anger and inviting God to deal with it.[5]

CRISIS PRAYER: *"In your anger do not sin. Do not let the sun go down while you are still angry, and do not give the devil a foothold."* (Ephesians 4:26)

"in your anger . . ." The word means irritate, or provoke and implies that one can be angry, but not sin. Jesus was angry when He found money-changers in the Temple, and when religious leaders threw an adulterous woman at His feet to try to get Him to contradict the law, but He was without sin. *"Do not sin"* is a quote from Psalm 4:4. Then Paul instructs us to not let the day end while we are still irritated, because that simply

gives the devil a *"foothold,"* which means you will not only remain angry all night but you will wake up the next day with the anger still a part of your feelings and actions.

1. Dear Lord, thank You for allowing me to experience anger, but thank You also for giving me the ability to be angry but not sin. Help me today to control my anger, especially as I :

2. In addition, Lord, I'd like to share the following with You:

Lord, it always seems we hurt
The ones we love most true.
Replace our anger with deeds of love
That can only come from You.

DAY TEN: HAVING PATIENCE

CRISIS CARE: Branson, Missouri was one of my mother's favorite places to travel. If you've never been to Branson, let me describe it to you: Just north of the Arkansas-Missouri state line, Branson is nestled in the Ozark Mountains, surrounded by an abundance of beautiful scenery. The town itself seems small until you turn west on Highway 76. Suddenly, you encounter a multitude of hotels, motels, restaurants, shops, and music theaters—lots of music theaters! Being a country music fan, my mother enjoyed seeing concerts there by the likes of Loretta Lynn, Mel Tillis, Glen Campbell, Roy Clark, Jim Stafford, and her favorite—Gene Watson. In addition to country singers, pop and gospel singers of my generation frequently can be found in Branson. We saw Bobby Vinton, Andy Williams, Pat and Debbie Boone, the Lennon Sisters, the Osmond Brothers, Dino Kartsanokis, and the Blackwoods—to name a few. And then there's Shoji Tabuchi: Every Branson veteran knows about Shoji and his spectacular theater, where even the restrooms are amazing!

Branson is great fun for music lovers, as well as shoppers and nature lovers. There's just one problem: Branson is home to the "world's longest parking lot." Well, it's not actually a parking lot; it's a highway! You see, at certain times of the day and night when the various shows are about to start or have just ended, more cars spill onto Highway 76 than it can handle. The lanes become overloaded, and the cars, trucks, RV's, and buses inch along at a snail's pace, sometimes coming to a complete halt. The city of Branson has worked hard, building secondary roads and alternate routes in recent years to accommodate the growing number of vehicles, but Branson regulars know that sometime during their visit, they're going to get stuck on

Highway 76. You know it; you plan for it; and you just make a point to allow enough time to be patient.

Caregiving can be like that, too. Caregivers learn that there will be times when too many things spill into their lives at one time. You know it; you plan for it; and you make a point to be patient. Easier said than done? Yes, when we try to do it on our own, but remember what Paul said about patience in Galatians 5. Paul identified "patience" as one of the fruit of the Spirit. In other words, when we let Him work in us, the Holy Spirit can produce patience in the Christian's life. Having patience is hard when we try to manufacture it by ourselves, but when we allow the Holy Spirit to enable and empower us, our lives can be characterized by patience, even when we find ourselves on overload!

CRISIS PRAYER: *"Better a patient man than a warrior, a man who controls his temper than one who takes a city."* (Proverbs 16:32)

Better is the *"patient,"* long suffering person, who retrains their thoughts, and *"controls . . . temper,"* and anger, than the valiant commander of a great army, who *"takes"* or captures, or occupies, a *"city."* While one overcomes external foes or obstacles; the other conquers self.

1. Dear Lord, thank You for assisting me in controlling my temper. Increase my patience today as I:

2. In addition, Lord, I'd like to share the following with You:

"Lord, give me patience and give it now!"
Too often I may say.
So, tie me up and slow me down
When I need time to pray.

DAY ELEVEN: MAINTAINING DIGNITY

CRISIS CARE: As we care for loved ones who are chronically ill, disabled, or elderly, one of the most important things we can do is to help maintain their dignity. Let me suggest a few ways—some learned from my own mistakes—to do so:

(1) Talk to them, not about them or for them. When a person has limitations requiring a caregiver, others have a tendency to talk in the third person (him, hers, they, etc.) as if the person were not in the room. When the loved one is present, whether it be at a family gathering, a doctor's appointment, or even in the hospital, it is important to talk in terms of "you" or "yours" rather than "him" or "hers." As much as possible, hear what the loved one has to say first, and then as necessary, the caregiver can give input.

(2) Watch the terminology we use as we provide care. For instance, I prefer not to use the term "adult diapers." Rather, terms such as "disposable underwear" or a brand name such as "Depends" sound more age-appropriate for adults.

(3) As much as possible, involve your loved one in decisions that affect him or her. Giving input on something as simple as what to have for supper or as important as a change in living arrangements validates his opinion and gives the loved one a sense of being an important part of the family.

(4) Don't assume your loved one no longer needs privacy. Studies have shown that caregivers often forget their loved ones' need for privacy, especially when their level of care involves significant assistance with personal hygiene and grooming.[1]

As always, Jesus is our example. He consistently treated people with dignity, no matter what their situation. Think about Zaccheus, a tax collector disdained by society, to whom Jesus said, *"I must go to your house today."* Remember the woman at the well, considered a social outcast among her people but treated with care and dignity by the Lord. Don't forget the man with leprosy who came to Jesus to be healed. While others kept their distance, Jesus reached out and touched the man. Treating others with dignity, compassion, and unconditional love is not a new idea. It was modeled perfectly for us by the One who loved us enough *"that while we were yet sinners, He died for us"* (Romans 5:8).

CRISIS PRAYER: *"She is clothed with strength and dignity; she can laugh at the days to come."* (Proverbs 31:25)

Interesting that even though this verse is about a female, the words *"strength"* and *"dignity,"* or honor are both masculine nouns in the original language. One can only assume in that day, the male was thought to be the stronger of the two, perhaps even the more honored, thus the writer of Proverbs is trying to elevate the role of woman. The word *"laugh"* goes back to the feminine, and means she can smile at the future. Some think this is a reference to the end times, but more probably it is a reference simply to tomorrow, the immediate future. She is not disquieted by any fear of what may happen, since she knows where her trust lies.

1. Dear Lord, thank You for equipping me with the strength and honor that allows me to smile at tomorrow. Now, help me today as I:

2. In addition, Lord, I'd like to share the following with You:

> *You never judge what's outside,*
> *But always look within.*
> *Help me, Lord, to see what is,*
> *But not forget what's been.*

DAY TWELVE: FINDING LAUGHTER

CRISIS CARE: I am not a morning person! Everyone who knows me well knows that fact to be true. On the other hand, my mother was an early-to-bed-early-to-rise person in her later years. She got up early because she wanted to; I got up early because I had to. As a result, I'm not much of a talker at the breakfast table. Not long after my mother came to live with us, we were having coffee together, and in an off-handed way of expressing my dislike of getting up early that day, I simply muttered, "Bluh!" Laughing, my mother responded with her own version of "bluh," and with those two utterances, we had a pretty good idea of how each of us felt that morning. As the days and weeks passed, our daily "bluhs" became a routine part of our early morning coffee with the frequency, intensity, and volume reflecting how we were feeling that morning. It was our own private joke, and even though it was silly, but it gave us something to laugh about, even on mornings when I didn't want to be awake or on days when she wasn't feeling particularly well.

For a long time, Reader's Digest has reminded us that "laughter is the best medicine," and there's a great deal of truth in that. In fact, Solomon said it first in Proverbs 17:22: *"A cheerful heart is good medicine, but a crushed spirit dries up the bones."* The importance of laughter in the life of both the caregiver and the care recipient is well-documented. Even during the Middle Ages, Henri de Mondeville, a professor of surgery, instructed, "Let the surgeon take care to regulate the whole regimen of the patient's life for joy and happiness, allowing his relatives and special friends to cheer him, and by having someone tell him jokes. The surgeon must forbid anger, hatred and sadness in the patient and remind him that the body grows fat from joy and thin from sadness."[1]

Several centuries later, Mark Twain concurred: "The human race has only one really effective weapon, and that's laughter. The moment it arises, all our harnesses yield, all our irritations and resentments slip away, and a sunny spirit takes their place." More recently, numerous studies have suggested that "there are positive effects to be gained from laughter as a great tension-releaser, pain reducer, breathing improver, and general elevator of moods."[2]

We are "fearfully and wonderfully made," and a part of God's design includes our bodies' physiological and psychological responses to laughter. Laughter does indeed affect the body, mind, and spirit. Thank you, Lord, for the gift of laughter!

CRISIS PRAYER: *"And Sarah said, "God hath made me to laugh, so that all who hear will laugh with me."* (Genesis 21:6 KJV)

Sarah, the wife of Abraham, said God made her *"to laugh"* so that others would join with her in laughter. Sarah's laugh was one of mingled emotions. Joy was uppermost in her mind, but ninety-year old women do not laugh for joy at the birth of a child. She had laughed earlier in Genesis 13:12, but that laughter was at the promise of a son. Now, having birthed the son, she laughs again. Note that no one would *"laugh"* at her, but they would *"laugh with"* her.

1. Dear Lord, thank You for the gift of laughter, although on some days, I don't feel like laughing. Help me today to be able to laugh, even as I:

2. In addition, Lord, I'd like to share the following with You:

Help us see the humor, Lord,
In things you bring our way.
Not laughing at but laughing with
Can brighten all our days.

DAY THIRTEEN: ACCEPTING CHANGE

CRISIS CARE: When parents grow older and need progressively increasing care, it is often the adult child who transitions into caregiver. In recent years, expressions such as "role reversal," "parenting the parent," and "parent-child turnabout" commonly have been used to describe this transition. However, some experts on aging have begun to question the use of these terms, as evidenced in this quote from Beverly Pfeiffer:

"The notion that child and parent are 'reversing roles' reflects misconceptions about aging and about caregiving…. Experts on aging suggest we reframe our thinking about dependence and independence in terms of the acceptance of another stage of development in life, rather than role reversal. This can help caregivers to accept their parent's need for help without treating them as children either in action or tone of voice."[1]

Nevertheless, accepting changes in the parent-child relationship is a part of the caregiving process. "It can be a difficult transition for a child to take on the role of . . . decision-maker," says Dr. Diana Kerwin of the Medical College of Wisconsin's Division of Geriatrics and Gerontology. The adult child "needs to be empowered to step in and begin caring for their ailing parent—making sure their parent takes his or her medication, for instance, or telling their parent they should not drive, and making difficult decisions about when the parent is no longer able to safely live alone."[2]

So, while the roles may not reverse, they do change, and this realization may generate a myriad of emotions in both the aging parent and the adult child. These emotions need to be recognized, acknowledged, and discussed, so that the changes can be accepted as another part of God's plan. As Linda Neukrug says in her Guidepost prayer, "Dear God, thank You for Your love that follows us throughout our lives. May I never lose my sense of wonder at how wonderfully You bring us from babyhood to adulthood."[3] God is there through all the ages and stages of our lives and the many changes that accompany them. With that knowledge, accepting those changes becomes a matter of faith rather than emotion.

CRISES PRAYER: *"Surely goodness and mercy shall follow me all the days of my life . . ."* (Psalm 23:6, Emphasis Added)

"Surely (an article of affirmation) *goodness and mercy* (kindness, piety, beauty) *shall follow me* (literally means to pursue or chase), so it puts the initiative on the part of *"goodness and mercy"* rather than on the part of the one being followed. As God's *"goodness and mercy"* have always followed him, the Psalmist has no doubt that they will continue while his life continues.

1. Dear Lord, thank You for always being with me in the changes of my life. Now, as life itself changes, would you continue to be with me, especially today as I:

2. In addition, Lord, I'd like to share the following with You:

"Thou shalt honor" does not cease

Just because we're grown.
May care be done with thoughtfulness
And reflect the love You've shown.

DAY FOURTEEN: HOLDING ON THROUGH THE ROUGH TIMES

CRISIS CARE: My great-niece Hannah took her first airplane flight at the age of five. As the plane climbed through the clouds toward cruising altitude, she excitedly told her mom and grandparents, "We're going up to where God is!" As they continued to climb, the plane suddenly encountered unexpected turbulence, at which point Hannah proclaimed, "I think we've already gone passed Him!" In her special five-year-old way, she had described her concept of God as a loving heavenly Father who keeps us safe from danger and harm. To her, the safety of being "where God is" did not match the turbulence she was feeling in that airplane.

As the now college senior continued to grow, she came to understand that life consists of both smooth flights and turbulent rides. Most recently, the COVID-19 crisis cancelled most of her senior year spring activities, and that heartbreak definitely was a "turbulent ride." Thankfully, though, God is there when things are smooth and when things get bumpy. As the Scriptures promise, nothing can separate us from His love.

Some care recipients have conditions, such as Alzheimer's, that may cause them to have good days and bad days. "A person with Alzheimer's can change from day-to-day, hour-to-hour, minute-to-minute.... They may be clear headed and cheerful in the morning, but confused, agitated and hostile by lunchtime," according to the Canadian Medical Association.[1] As a result, the caregiver's "ride" can be smooth one day and turbulent the next. It is a blessing to know that no matter how much turbulence we face, we can never get bumped beyond "where God is." As the psalmist wrote, *"If I go up to the heavens, you are there; if I make my bed in the depths, you are there. If I rise on the wings of the dawn, if I settle on the far side of the sea, even there your hand will guide me, your right hand will hold me fast"* (Psalm 139:8–10). When things are smooth, don't forget to thank Him for His constant presence, but when things get bumpy, don't hesitate to hang on tight to His strong and loving hand!

CRISIS PRAYER: *"For I am convinced that neither death nor life, neither angels nor demons, neither the present nor the future, nor any powers, neither height nor depth, nor anything else in all creation, will be able to separate us from the love of God that is in Christ Jesus our Lord."* (Romans 8:38–39)

The listing in these verses is intended to include every possible category of being, especially those unseen powers of evil against which the warfare of the Christian was more particularly directed. Paul was *"convinced"* that no powers or circumstances whatever, would ever separate us from the love of God, which is in Christ Jesus our Lord, nor bar our attainment of our final inheritance.

1. Dear Lord, thank You for the assurance that nothing, not even the rough times, can ever separate me from You. That is especially helpful today as I:

2. In addition, Lord, I'd like to share the following with You:

*Thank you for the good times,
And thanks when things get rough.
It's then You hold us tighter,
So we know Your strength's enough.*

DAY FIFTEEN: BEING SATISFIED ... NOT "SANDWICHED"

CRISIS CARE: In the world of caregiving, there is a distinct group sometimes referred to as the "sandwich generation." These are mostly those between the age of forty-five and fifty-five who are caring for both their parents and their children. Since this term was coined by Carol Abaya, much has been written about the pressures of managing both children and aging parents and the various techniques used to cope with the stress of being "in the middle."

Recently, AARP conducted a national study of this population to learn their characteristics, feelings, and coping mechanisms, and received rather unexpected responses from the so-called "Me Generation."

"The results of the study are intriguing, and even surprising," AARP reports. "They show a generation who tell us that family is the most important thing in their lives. Respondents said they welcome the opportunity to be involved in the care of their loved ones…. They are generally comfortable with their family roles, and self-confident as they manage the dual responsibilities of parents and children."[1] In other words, these caregivers are feeling satisfied rather than sandwiched.

Perhaps AARP found these results somewhat surprising because feelings of satisfaction can be elusive—both in our emotional and our spiritual selves. We might call it the "Grass-Is-Always-Greener Syndrome." Nevertheless, the Bible gives us guidance on how to become and remain spiritually satisfied. Here are some of those whom God has promised in His Word to satisfy:

1. The meek who seek -- *"The meek shall eat and be satisfied: they shall praise the Lord that seek him...."* (Psalm 22:26 KJV).

2. The just who trust -- *"How excellent is thy lovingkindness, O God! therefore the children of men put their trust under the shadow of thy wings. They shall be abundantly satisfied...."* (Psalm 36:7–8 KJV).

3. Those who praise all their days -- *"Thus will I bless thee while I live: I will lift up my hands in thy name. My soul shall be satisfied as with marrow and fatness; and my mouth shall praise thee with joyful lips"* (Psalm 63:4–5 KJV); *"Satisfy us in the morning with your unfailing love, that we may sing for joy and be glad all our days"* (Psalm 90:14).

4. Those who call when they fall -- *"Because he loves me, says the Lord, I will rescue him; I will protect him, for he acknowledges my name. He will call upon me, and I will answer him; I will be with him in trouble, I will deliver him and honor him. With long life will I satisfy him and show him my salvation"*

(Psalm 91:14–16).

CRISIS PRAYER: *"The fear of the Lord leads to life; and he who has it will abide in satisfaction; he will not be visited with evil."* (Proverbs 19:23 NKJV)

The *"fear"* or reverence of the Lord leads to *"life"* – a masculine noun, meaning alive, fresh, strong *"life."* The word used for *"abide"* means to stop, to stay permanently, to rest content in *"satisfaction."* The New Testament offers a higher blessing than, *"not be visited with evil,"* by offering protection, not only from evil, but also protection in the midst of it.

1. Dear Lord, thank You for strong life that allows for me to be protected by You. I ask You to protect me today, especially as I:

2. In addition, Lord, I'd like to share the following with You:

Lord, You know I'm satisfied
With all You did and how You died
From sin and shame to set us free!
But are you satisfied with me?

DAY SIXTEEN: PUTTING ON THE ARMOR

CRISIS CARE: As a preteen, my nephew Zach decided he wanted to learn to play ice hockey. During the first dozen or so lessons, the only equipment required was his helmet. Once he reached "Hockey 3" lessons, however, he was required to wear full gear. As we helped him locate, purchase, and put on the equipment for the first time, we gained a new appreciation for hockey players. They wear a lot of stuff under those uniforms. There are the shoulder pads, which protect not only the shoulders, but also the chest and upper back. There are thick padded pants, elbow pads, shin guards, a neck cover and, for lack of a better term, a hockey jockey. Add to all of that a pair of thick padded gloves, ankle-to-knee socks, the helmet with a metal face cage, and the ice skates, and only then is the hockey player ready to pick up his offensive weapon—the hockey stick. Especially in youth hockey, the players must prepare themselves in all the appropriate protective gear before they can ever take their stand on the ice.

In a spiritual sense, God instructs Christians to do something very similar. In Ephesians 6, Paul tells us to put on the full armor of God so that we can take our stand against Satan's schemes, and then he specifies the pieces of armor -- our spiritual "equipment" -- to put on. Notice the order: first, the belt of truth, the breastplate of righteousness, the "shoes" of readiness, the shield of faith, and the helmet of salvation. Then, after we have prepared ourselves with our "protective gear," we are to take up the only offensive weapon Paul mentions – *"the sword of the Spirit, which is the word of God."* [Emphasis Added]. As Christians, we must prepare ourselves in all the appropriate spiritual armor so that when the devil attacks, we will be able to *"stand our ground"* and *"extinguish all the flaming arrows of the evil one."*

For us as caregivers, what are some of the *"flaming arrows"* the evil one may decide to throw our way? In the words of the Alzheimer's Association, here are a few: Depression ("I just don't care anymore"), anxiety ("What happens when he needs more care than I can give?"), anger ("If she asks me that same question one more time, I'll scream!"), social withdrawal ("I just don't have the energy to get together with our neighbors anymore"), and health problems ("I can't remember the last time I felt good").[1] Thankfully, Paul assures us that we can extinguish these flaming arrows with the shield of faith, and we can fight back with our spiritual sword, which is the Word of God.

CRISIS PRAYER: *"Be strong in the Lord and in His mighty power. Put on the full armor of God so that you can take your stand against the devil's schemes."* (Ephesians 6:10–11)

"Be strong in the Lord, and in the power of his might." Compare with Ephesians 3:16, where the heavenly provision for obtaining strength is specified. The ever-recurring formula, "*in the Lord,*" indicates the relation to Christ in which alone the strength can be experienced. The might is Christ's, but by faith it becomes our strength. To be *"strong"* is our duty; to be weak is our sin. Chained to a soldier, the apostle's mind would focus naturally to the subject of armor and warfare. Put on armor, for life is a battle-field, not a scene of soft enjoyment and ease, but of hard conflict, with foes within and without. Then we are told to *"put on"* as we would clothe ourselves, with the *"full armor,"* not partial armor, but be completely and adequately armed in order to *"stand against the devil's schemes,"* that is the wiles of the devil a technical term applied to the most skillful enemies. Our

chief enemy does not engage us in open warfare but deals in wiles and *"schemes."*

1. Dear Lord, thank You for equipping me for life, which often seems to be a battle with Satan. I need Your armor today, especially as I:

2. In addition, Lord, I'd like to share the following with You:

The devil is an evil coward
Seeking whom he may devour,
So help me keep my armor ready,
Shield held high, and sword held steady.

DAY SEVENTEEN: SAYING "NO"

CRISIS CARE: Saying "no" can be one of the most difficult tasks for a caregiver, especially when the care recipient is a parent. Brenda Jones Vieregg, one of the authors of *Fourteen Friends' Guide to Eldercaring*, identified part of the problem in this way: "The reason eldercaring is so difficult is that, besides the physical work which we all can do when you're caring for somebody, it involves the longest relationship of our whole life. And so you bring all of the emotions of that relationship into the caring process."[1] Yet, setting limits by saying "no" is sometimes necessary in the caregiving relationship for at least two reasons.

First, saying "no" is vital when it's in the best interest of the loved one receiving care. Illness, disability, or the aging process may cause the care recipient to have unrealistic expectations or the desire to participate in activities that are no longer appropriate. A common example is driving after it is no longer safe for the loved one to do so. Even though it's difficult, the adult child, adult sibling, or caregiving spouse needs to say "no" for the safety and well-being of the care recipient as well as others.

Additionally, setting limits by saying "no" is sometimes necessary for the physical and emotional well-being of the caregiver. Finding a balance in taking care of your loved one and taking care of yourself can be tricky. "Your care receiver may need constant reassurance about his/her safety, your love, medical care or costs, changes in your life together… or any other number of personal concerns. Your ability to listen to their concerns is important," caregiving experts advise. On the other hand, "all caregivers should receive respite regularly. Give yourself permission to ask for help. Turn to other people for help—your family, friends, church/synagogue, and neighbors.

Allow yourself a break from your caregiving responsibilities."[2] Accomplishing this may mean saying "no" — even to a parent — without feeling guilty.

Perhaps it will help to remember that even our loving heavenly Father sometimes says "no" to our requests. Unlimited by time and space, our omniscient, omnipresent God sees the big picture, and because of His unconditional love, He acts in our best interest by sometimes saying "no" or "wait" or "not right now" to our prayers.

Therein lies the secret to saying "no" appropriately as a caregiver: look at the big picture, decide what's in the best interest of those involved, and act with unconditional love.

CRISIS PRAYER: *"Going a little farther, he fell with his face to the ground and prayed, 'My Father, if it is possible, may this cup be taken from me. Yet not as I will, but as you will.'"* (Matthew 26:39)

"He fell" tells us how intense this prayer of Jesus was. He did not bow His head and close His eyes. He did not kneel to pray. *"He fell with His face to the ground,"* and He addressed the prayer to His *"Father,"* which is the only direction to offer a crisis prayer. Mark remembers that Jesus prayed *"Abba, Father"* which is the Hebrew child's term of endearment for the father. Jesus reviewed His options, *"If it is possible,"* and yielded to the will of the Father – *"as You will."* In other words, the answer to the prayer request of Jesus was, "No." The writer of Hebrews gives great insight into this crisis prayer (Hebrews 5:7-8).

1. Dear Lord, thank You for the role model you gave of being able to say "No" to requests. Please help me today as I try to give the proper answers to the requests that came my way, especially:

2. In addition, Lord, I'd like to share the following with You:

> *"Take this cup if it be Your will,"*
> *In agony Christ prayed.*
> *Help us accept the "no's" as well*
> *As He did on that day.*

DAY EIGHTEEN: FINDING BEAUTY

CRISIS CARE: Today's devotional consists of the words to a song I wrote several years ago. They will probably be most meaningful to those who are caregivers for children with disabilities, but I believe there is meaning to be found by any caregiver.

Butterflies and Rainbows

Said the caterpillar to the lovely butterfly,

"Why aren't you ugly like me?

You have beautiful colors, you can

soar in the sky

And I can only crawl on this tree."

But the butterfly replied, "Keep on

climbing that tree.

Keep working and doing your best.

Keep reaching for the sky, my friend,

and you will see

Time will take care of the rest."

Said the dark, rainy cloud to the bright sunshine,

"Why aren't you ugly like me?

You can brighten up the world; you

can make it fine,

And I can only cry constantly."

But the sunshine replied, "Come along with me.

We'll work together wherever we go.

Add your sparkle to my glowing, friend,

and you will see.

We'll paint the skies with lovely rainbows."

Said that special child to others all around,

"Why aren't you ugly like me?

You can learn; you can walk;

and it gets me down . . .

All the things I can't do easily."

But a friend reaches out her hand and

says with a smile,

"Let me show you all the things you can do.

Keep reaching for the sky, my friend,

and in a while,

We'll find the butterflies and

rainbows in you."

CRISIS PRAYER: *"He has made everything beautiful in its time. He has also set eternity in the hearts of men; yet they cannot fathom what God has done from beginning to end."* (Ecclesiastes 3:11)

"He has made everything…" means, the whole, all, any. The fact that we are told that it is all made *"in its time"* reminds us that everything that happens in God's will, happens in *"the fullness of time."* Setting *"eternity* (some translations say *"world") in the hearts of men"* means God has placed it in the feelings, the will, the intellect, center of mankind, yet they *"cannot fathom"* God's works. We can only see minute parts of the great whole;

we cannot comprehend all in one view, cannot understand the law that regulates the time and season of every circumstance.

1. Dear Lord, thank You for knowing and seeing more than I do, but also for allowing me to see the beauty in Your creation, especially today as I:

2. In addition, Lord, I'd like to share the following with You:

Help me see the butterflies
And not the old cocoon.
Help me find the rainbows, Lord,
For they are gone so soon.

DAY NINETEEN: PUTTING THE PIECES TOGETHER

CRISIS CARE: Between the time my father retired in 1979 and went to be with the Lord in 1988, he completed a large number of jigsaw puzzles. Not being one to just sit and watch TV, he always seemed to have a puzzle going on a card table in the den. We didn't realize how many though until after his death, when we found a large stack of puzzles separated by poster board under his bed. Recently, therefore, hearing a luncheon speaker use a jigsaw puzzle analogy reminded me of my Dad . . . not just because of the puzzles themselves, but also the lessons learned from them.[1] I decided that "lessons from a jigsaw puzzle" had something to say to caregivers, as well.

1. *Establish the border first.* In puzzles and in caregiving, boundaries are necessary and important.
2. *Don't force a fit.* Forcing someone or something to fit where it doesn't belong may be a temporary solution but will usually cause problems in the long run.
3. *Look at the big picture and don't get bogged down with the little pieces.* It's easy sometimes to lose sight of the forest for the trees.
4. *When nothing seems to come together, take a break.* Things often look different when you come back to them.
5. *Doing it right takes time.* Putting all the pieces together correctly can be a lengthy process. Don't rush or become impatient.
6. *Pieces can fall apart without the proper glue.* To avoid falling to pieces, depend on the "glue" that holds our lives together . . . friends *"who stick closer than a brother"* and

the special Friend we have in Jesus. (Proverbs 18:24 Emphasis Added).

7. *Follow the guide given by the creator.* The creator of a puzzle provides a picture of the finished product to use as a guide. Our Creator also provides a Guide to follow for those *"who receive the word with all readiness of mind, and search the scriptures daily"* (Acts 17:11 KJV).

8. *One missing piece makes a difference.* It takes all the pieces to complete the picture. The proverb says, *"It takes the whole village to raise a child."* In like manner, caregiving often needs to be a team effort by family, friends, church, and community.

CRISIS PRAYER: *"And when she hath found it she calleth her friends and her neighbors together, saying, "Rejoice with me; for I have found the **piece** which I had lost."* (Luke 15:9 KJV Emphasis Added)

"Rejoice with me" means congratulate me, and sometimes it means sympathize with me. I "*found the piece*" is a good translation for applying to the puzzle analogy. However, the word literally means, *drachma,* a Greek silver coin, which still, was a "piece" of her possessions. "*I lost*" strikes a difference from the preceding parable of the lost sheep, in which it was the sheep that got lost on its own. Here it is the woman who lost the object. The parable gives us a glimpse of God himself, rejoicing with His own, and with His angels over the salvation of a single person.

1. Dear Lord, thank You helping me put all the pieces together, especially today as I:

2. In addition, Lord, I'd like to share the following with You:

We juggle all the pieces, Lord,
And try to make them fit.
Help us see the big design,
Press on, and never quit.

DAY TWENTY: ENCOURAGING INDEPENDENCE

CRISIS CARE: Very early in my work with special-needs students, I encountered the term "learned helplessness." I grasped the meaning when my supervisor pointed out to me that in my eagerness to assist students, I was doing too much for them. I was doing things they could do, or at least could learn to do, because I was uncomfortable watching them having to work so hard or struggle with a skill. My supervisor wisely helped me realize that in these instances, I was actually doing a disservice rather than helping because the struggle was a part of the learning process. By doing too much, I was teaching the students to depend on others rather than gaining independence.

The same concept comes into play in rehabilitation after illness or injury. Have you ever watched a physical therapist or an occupational therapist as they work with their clients? As family members, we often want to do for the patient, but the therapists' approach is to provide treatment and accommodations so that the patient can do for himself. Why? So that the patient can regain or maintain the highest level of independence possible for as long as possible.

Caregivers need to keep the concept of "learned helplessness" in mind as we seek to find a balance between under-care and over-care. When we provide support and empathy instead of over-involvement, we encourage our loved ones to maintain as much independence as they can for as long as possible.

Just the opposite is true, however, in our walk with the Lord. Learning to be dependent on Him is one of the most important aspects of our spiritual growth. The more we try to do on our own, the more likely we are to experience frustration, confusion, and failure. The more we submit to His will and depend on Him for direction, the more likely we are to experience peace, assurance, and blessings in our lives. In Psalm 62, David wrote, *"My salvation and my honor depend on God. He is my mighty rock, my refuge. Trust in him at all times, O people; pour out your hearts to him, for God is our refuge."* We are helpless without Him, but when we stand "empty-handed before God in total dependence and self-surrender," we find our strength.

CRISIS PRAYER: *"Trust in the Lord with all your heart, and lean not to your own understanding. In all your ways acknowledge him, and he will make your paths straight."* (Proverbs 3:5–6)

To *"trust"* means to be confident and sure. *"With all your heart"* means with the feelings, the will, and the intellect. *"Lean not"* means not to rest upon, just as a person rests upon a cane for support. It is derived from the practice of kings who were accustomed to appearing in public leaning on their friends and ministers. To *"acknowledge Him"* means He will *"make your paths straight"* or as earlier translations say, *"He will direct your path."* (KJV)

1. Dear Lord, thank You for being so trustworthy, that I can trust You. I need to trust You today to give me direction as I try to balance encouragement and discouragement, especially as I:

2. In addition, Lord, I'd like to share the following with You:

Lord, independence is a need
Our human nature seeks.
Help me surrender "self" to You,
For You have blessed the meek.

DAY TWENTY-ONE: EVALUATING YOURSELF

CRISIS CARE: What kind of caregiver are you? What is your caregiving style? Is yours a healthy caregiving relationship? The Caregiver's Self-Rating Scale from the San Diego Mental Health Services is a ten-point continuum which describes the various styles of caregiving, ranging from abandonment to fusion of personalities (see Appendix A). Caregivers can place themselves on the scale to determine how they value the care receiver and how they value themselves.

Take a moment to review the Scale on pages 130–131, and place yourself on the continuum based on the description that sounds most like you. Hopefully, you've identified yourself somewhere in the middle. The low numbers give little or no value to the care receiver, while the high numbers give little or no value to your own needs as an individual. Neither extreme is healthy in the caregiving relationship. Finding yourself at either end of the continuum may be an indication that you need to take action through a support group or counselor.

The Self-Rating Scale is a simple yet meaningful way to evaluate ourselves as caregivers, but how should we evaluate ourselves as Christians? In the first chapter of 2 Peter, there's a simple yet meaningful way to evaluate our spiritual growth. Simon Peter tells us that our goal is to *"participate in the divine nature,"* — to be like Jesus. Then he gives us a "checklist" of sorts: *"Make every effort to add to your faith, goodness; and to goodness, knowledge; and to knowledge, self-control; and to self-control, perseverance; and to perseverance, godliness; and to godliness, brotherly kindness; and to brotherly kindness, love. For if you possess these qualities in increasing measure, they will keep you from being <u>ineffective</u> and <u>unproductive</u> in your knowledge of our Lord Jesus*

Christ" (2 Peter 1:5–8 EMPHASIS ADDED). There it is . . . an eight-point "checklist" to evaluate our effectiveness and productivity as we seek to become more and more like Him.

Which of these qualities do you possess? Are you experiencing them *"in increasing measure?"* Which do you need to add through His divine power?

Are you, as Paul is in 2 Corinthians 3:18, *"being transformed into his likeness with ever-increasing glory, which comes from the Lord, who is the Spirit?"*

CRISIS PRAYER: *"Examine yourselves to see whether you are in the faith; test yourselves. Do you not realize that Christ Jesus is in you—unless, of course, you fail the test?"* (2 Corinthians 13:5)

"Examine yourselves." The Greek word, *peirazete* means to try or to test yourself, and it is present, active, imperative. The imperative mood conveys a command for someone to perform the action of the verb, *"examine."* The present tense gives it an ongoing aspect. In other words, we are to keep on examining ourselves. *"Test yourselves,"* also present, active, imperative, meaning continue to seek approval. If you rate poorly on the exam and *"fail the test"* then obviously, Christ is not *"in you."*

1. Dear Lord, thank You for helping me study for the test. May my ranking be acceptable to You, equipping me to serve effectively today, especially as I:

2. In addition, Lord, I'd like to share the following with You:

We've heard that we're the only Bible
Some will ever read.
Lord, make us more like You so they
Can find the Word they need.

DAY TWENTY-TWO: USING WORDS CONSTRUCTIVELY

CRISIS CARE: For many years, my summers included several Christian children's camps, where I generally led music and fun time. One of the campers' perennial favorites went like this, from an unknown author:

> I've got this tongue I can't control.
>
> It's a fight that I can't win.
>
> I've got this tongue I can't control,
>
> And it leads me into sin.
>
> So I give it to you, my Lord.
>
> Help it laugh and sing and pray,
>
> And may it never, never, never, ever
>
> Stick out at my brother.
>
> That's my gift to You today!

What made this song especially enjoyable for the campers were the sound effects made by wagging the tongue between lines. We had a lot of fun with the song, but it also reminded campers and adult sponsors how easy it is to use the tongue—God's gift of speech—in a hurtful way. It was a lesson we all could use, especially while spending a week together in close communion during the 100+ degree Texas heat.

Of course, this little song was a playful way of teaching the serious lesson we find in the third chapter of James. He compares the tongue to the bit in a horse's mouth, the rudder of a ship, and the spark that starts a forest fire—small items that can cause big things to happen. James reminds us that while humans have tamed almost every animal, we have not been successful taming the tongue. He decries the fact that we praise God and curse God's creation with the same tongue.

Let's think about how this lesson applies to the caregiving relationship in both positive and negative ways. First the negative: Harsh or angry words, criticism, and any communication that puts down rather than lifts up need to be avoided by the caregiver. It's easy to become impatient and say something that we really don't mean or that we will regret later. Caregivers need to be tuned in to this possibility and be careful to put the brain in gear before we put the mouth in motion.

Now, the positive: Our little song makes three good suggestions—laugh, sing, and pray. We have already discussed the importance of laughter and music in previous daily readings, but this will serve as a reminder. Praying with or for the care recipient is another excellent way to use the gift of speech in a positive manner. Reading to the care receiver can help keep communication and thinking skills functioning better and longer. I recently read a review of a book on eldercare, and the reviewer made the observation that while the book had many good suggestions, it completely omitted any reference to reading the Bible and how singing the "old hymns" to aging loved ones often can be soothing and reassuring.

Finally, make opportunities to use words to build people up, strengthen self-esteem, and acknowledge their accomplishments by implementing an old rule-of-thumb used by teachers . . . give at least four positives for every negative. Then you are using your words constructively, as the Lord intended.

CRISIS PRAYER: *"Do not let any unwholesome talk come out of your mouths, but only what is helpful for building others up according to their needs, that it may benefit those who listen."* (Ephesians 4:29)

"*Unwholesome*" is the Greek word *sapros,* meaning rotten, useless, corrupt, depraved vs. words that are helpful for "*building others up*"– a word that has to do with architecture, as in building a structure. The "*unwholesome*" word is forbidden, not just because it defiles the speaker's soul, and is an offence to God, but because it is a sin against others, pulling down instead of building them up. So, we are to build up others according to their "*needs*" which obviously everyone has a different mixture. However, as we uniquely speak words that build others up, we "*benefit those who listen.*" Some translations use the word "*grace*" in place of the word "*benefit*" – "*give grace to those who hear*" (NASB). The words of the caregiver should ever focus on improvement or edification.

1. Lord, please let the "*words of my mouth and the meditation of my heart be acceptable in Your sight*" (Psalm 19:14, NASB) and also in the hearing of those around me today, especially:

2. In addition, Lord, I'd like to share the following with You:

> *Help me laugh and sing and pray*
> *With all the words I use today.*
> *Help me build up and not put down*
> *Every time I make a sound.*

DAY TWENTY-THREE: RECHARGING YOUR BATTERIES

CRISIS CARE: You board an airplane and settle into your seat. As the plane leaves the gate, the flight attendant begins to recite the safety instructions given at the beginning of every flight. "In the unlikely event that our cabin loses pressure, an oxygen mask will drop in front of you," the flight attendant demonstrates. "If you are traveling with a child or another person who needs assistance, secure your own mask first, and then help the one who needs assistance." At first blush, that instruction may sound selfish or even foolish. After all, a parent's natural reaction in a crisis is to come to the aid of her child first, even if that means putting herself in danger. Upon further reflection, however, the instructions make perfect sense. We are not being told to take care of our own needs instead of another's. Rather, the airlines are reminding us to take care of ourselves first so that we will be able to take care of others.

That is a reminder that we need as caregivers, as well. Caregivers must give themselves permission to nurture themselves without guilt and with as much compassion as they reserve for others. "Figure out what your needs are," urges Professor Alice Domar of the Harvard Medical School. "Then figure out how others in your life can help you meet each need. Each morning think about something you might do for yourself that day. Remember: If you don't care for yourself, you're less able to care for others."[1]

Even Jesus found it necessary to withdraw from the pressing crowds on occasion. In Luke 5, we are told that after teaching the people who pressed upon him to hear the word of God, *after performing miracles and calling disciples, and after healing many sicknesses, "Jesus withdrew himself into the wilderness, and prayed"* (Luke 5:16 KJV). In today's vernacular, Jesus needed time to "recharge His spiritual batteries" after ministering to the multitudes. Jesus was God, but He was God in a human body that needed physical, emotional, and spiritual renewal at times. Why should we feel inadequate when we experience the same kind of needs? Find ways to "recharge your batteries," and then find time to do those things. Remember: A "dead battery" doesn't do anybody much good, but a fully charged battery can keep going and going and going . . .!

CRISIS PRAYER: *"The apostles gathered around Jesus and reported to him all they had done and taught. Then, because so many people were coming and going that they did not even have a chance to eat, he said to them, 'Come with me by yourselves to a quiet place and get some rest.' So they went away by themselves in a boat to a solitary place."* (Mark 6:30–32)

The combination of the disciples reporting to Him *"all they had done and taught"* and the people *"coming and going"* apparently had a physical effect on Jesus, to the extent that they had not had a *"chance to eat."* In other words, they were so intent on ministering to others that they had forgotten to take care of their own needs. So Jesus doesn't send them away to rest, but led them away. They went to a *"solitary"* (from the Greek word, *eremon*) place, meaning literally, a lonesome place. Some translations call it a *"desert place"* and others *"a deserted place"* and Luke 9:10 identifies it as *"Bethsaida"* which was also known as "fish village."

1. Dear Lord, thank You for your model and Your encouragement to get away and take care of ourselves. Today, I especially need to:

2. In addition, Lord, I'd like to share the following with You:

Lord, take me to a quiet place
To be alone with You.
Renew my heart and soul and mind
And give me strength anew.

DAY TWENTY-FOUR: WORKING TOGETHER FOR GOOD

CRISIS CARE: Where were you on September 11, 2001? What were you doing on November 22, 1963? If you are old enough to remember, who were you with on December 7, 1941? Some dates are indelibly stamped into our memories by tragedies such as the 9/11 attacks, the Kennedy assassination, and Pearl Harbor. For my former church, Wedgwood Baptist in Fort Worth, September 15, 1999, is such a date. On that evening, a disturbed gunman walked into a "See You After the Pole" youth meeting and began firing. Fourteen people were shot, seven died, and many more were traumatized before the shooter turned his gun on himself. It was a dark night for our church family. I remember sleep did not come easily for me that night after learning a choir friend had been killed, a friend from work had been wounded, and another co-worker had lost her daughter. When I awoke early the next morning, I immediately turned on the television, and the local stations were interviewing our pastor, Dr. Al Meredith. As the sun rose over the scene of such darkness, I remember Brother Al quoting Scripture as a part of his response to the media, stating that while our hearts were heavy with sorrow, we would not *"grieve like the rest of men, who have no hope."* (1 Thessalonians 4:13) Proclaiming "we will not let the powers of darkness overcome the power of light," he was able to witness to the television audience as he continued to respond to the reporters' questions.

The local audience became a national audience as he appeared on network news and programs such as Larry King's. But this was only the beginning of God's fulfillment of His promise in Romans 8:28: *"And we know that in all things God works for the good of those who love him, who have been called according to his purpose."* It would take a book to record all the ways the Lord used people involved in this tragedy to lead others to salvation and to minister to people literally throughout the world. Perhaps Campus Crusade for Christ founder Dr. Bill Bright said it best: "Only God can turn a tearful tragedy into a glorious victory."[1]

As mentioned in Day One, caregiving often begins with a tragedy -- an unwelcomed diagnosis, a life-altering injury, a grim prognosis, or even the death of a previous caregiver. And so, when faced with such crises, how should Christian caregivers respond? Author Verdell Davis offers this suggestion: "Most often we cannot choose what happens to us -- our choice lies in what we do with what life brings our way.... The pains, the heartaches, the losses of our lives can become the altar on which we offer up to God all the things that keep us relying on our own strength. It is then that God can truly do a new work in us and show us Himself in ways we have never seen before."[2]

In his second letter to the Corinthians, Paul stated it this way: *"But the Lord said to me, 'My grace is sufficient for you, for my power is made perfect in weakness.' Therefore, I will boast all the more gladly about my weaknesses so that Christ's power may rest on me"* (2 Corinthians 12:9–10). Only through the power of Jesus Christ can we experience hope and victory amid tragedy.

CRISIS PRAYER: *"Be strong and courageous. Do not be afraid or terrified because of them, for the Lord your God goes with you; he will never leave you nor forsake you."* (Deuteronomy 31:6 NIV)

The word for *"strong"* means to fasten upon, to seize, to bind, restrain, or conquer. The word *"courageous"* means to be stout, strong, bold, or alert. To possess these two characteristics would allow one not to be *"afraid"* or *"terrified."* Further, there is the promise that God *"goes with you"* that is goes equally with you, plus He will *"will never leave you nor forsake you."* Moses assures Israel of the constant presence of God with them. This promise, though made at this time particularly to Israel and to Joshua, yet belongs to all believers of future generations.

1. Dear Lord, thank You for the assurance of Your presence even in the darkest of times and in the worst of tragedies. Do not forsake me today, especially as I:

2. In addition, Lord, I'd like to share the following with You:

> *The night is darkest just before dawn,*
> *But soon we see the Light has come.*
> *Rejoicing begins and weeping is gone*
> *When You're the One we lean upon.*

DAY TWENTY-FIVE: STAYING PUT

CRISIS CARE: Aging in place is a relatively new term used to describe the trend of continuing to live in the community as independently as possible. According to the Blue Cross and Blue Shield of Texas *LifeTimes* publication, this phenomenon has become so prevalent that designers and builders have begun not only to take notice, but also to take action. In fact, the National Association of Home Builders (NAHB) now offers a three-day certification course for members who want to increase their knowledge of "barrier-free" living environments, as well as the design implications of aging.[1]

Certified Aging in Place Specialists are trained to look ahead to difficulties each of us might encounter as we age so that homes and apartments can be built or remodeled to meet those needs. Their recommendations frequently include such elements as (1) hallways and doors wide enough to accommodate wheelchairs, (2) low-rise thresholds, (3) kitchen counter heights that allow for sitting down while working, (4) non-slip flooring or low density carpet, (5) at least one downstairs bedroom and bath, (6) easy-to-reach and easy-to-read thermostats, and (7) bathrooms prepared for the easy addition of grab bars when needed.

"As we get older, most of us would prefer to be at home where things are familiar," states Mary Jo Peterson, president of a Connecticut consulting firm that specializes in barrier-free design.[2] Now, more than ever, designers and builders can make it not just possible, but easy to age in place . . . to stay put as we mature.

Maturing as a Christian sometimes involves staying put, as well. While we are frequently instructed in the Scriptures to "*go*," we are sometimes called upon to "wait." Perhaps the best known of these verses is Isaiah 40:31 (KJV): *"But they that wait upon the Lord shall renew their strength; they shall mount up with wings as eagles; they shall run, and not be weary; and they shall walk, and not faint."*

Why are we sometimes called upon to wait during our Christian walk? I am reminded of my days in high school and college marching bands. As a half-time performance unfolded, our task was usually to move down the field— eight steps for every five yards, in time with the music. Sometimes, however, the band director would instruct some of us to "march in place" so that our legs were moving, but we weren't going anywhere. Why? We were part of his bigger plan, and while we marched in place, the movement all around us would eventually converge into a design or a word that was clear to those watching in the stands. Then, when the time was right, we would move on to the next element in the program.

"Marching in place" as Christians is sometimes necessary so the Lord can work all around us to make clear His bigger plan. Then in the *"fullness of time,"* He will reveal to us when we should move forward and what our next step should be. In the meantime, He will use that wait-time to renew our strength so that when He says "go," we will be ready to *"run and not be weary."*

CRISIS PRAYER: *"Wait on the Lord: be of good courage, and he shall strengthen thine heart: wait, I say, on the Lord."* (Psalm 27:14 KJV)

"Wait on the Lord." The preposition *"on"* means to wait with or to wait near. We are not waiting at a great distance, but close by, and as we *"wait"* we are to do so with *"good courage,"*

meaning brave, strong, bold, stout. *"He shall strengthen"* means you are to make an effort to be strong, and the strength will be given, as you make the effort. Then in this strength, continue to *"wait."*

1. Dear Lord, thank You for making it all right to slow down, and even *"wait."* I will need Your strength today, especially as I:

2. In addition, Lord, I'd like to share the following with You:

May we always walk with You
Because we know Your steps are true.
Help us walk the way You've said,
Not lag behind or run ahead.

DAY TWENTY-SIX: WALKING TOWARD THE LIGHT

CRISIS CARE: As a young adult, I served as the youth or children's director for several churches in central Texas. Since our youth activities often lasted longer than other church activities, I sometimes found myself turning off lights and locking up the church building after everyone else had gone. At one church, I dreaded a particular hallway on those occasions because of the location of the light switch. Turning the light on when arriving or turning it off when leaving required a trek down the dark hall while it was illuminated only by a small emergency light. When entering to turn on the light, I walked toward the emergency light and could see where I was going and what I was doing. However, after switching it off and turning to leave, I was no longer facing the emergency light, and the same hallway seemed dark and potentially hazardous. What made the difference? It was whether or not I was walking toward the light.

Someone has said that placing our faith in the Lord is like driving at night with headlights. An automobile's lights give just enough illumination to drive a certain distance down the road. The driver cannot see beyond that point but must drive to the edge of the darkness to project more light. This same concept is captured in Psalm 119:105, where God's Word is described as a *"lamp unto my feet,"* not a spotlight to the far end of the road. When we walk toward the Light with faith, He will always light our path enough to see what our next step should be.

Caregiving is often characterized by uncertainties. What does the future hold? Am I making the right decisions for my loved one? Can I do this alone? For how long? Will our finances hold out? Should we stay here or move? How will my decisions affect other family members? And the list of questions goes on and on....

As we face the uncertainties that accompany caregiving, walking toward the Light becomes especially important. I'm reminded of the old gospel song that says,

> Many things about tomorrow
>
> I don't seem to understand,
>
> But I know Who holds the future
>
> And I know Who holds my hand.[1]

When the future seems uncertain, remember that the One who holds the future firmly in His hands stands ready to guide each step we take. When we walk toward the Light and grasp His hand in faith, He will *"show us the path of life"* . . . one step at a time (Psalm 16:11).

CRISIS PRAYER: *"I will praise the Lord, who counsels me; even at night my heart instructs me. . . . You have made known to me the path of life; you will fill me with joy in your presence, with eternal pleasures at your right hand."* (Psalm 16:7, 11)

"Who counsels me. . ." means one who advises, deliberates, or resolves, and they do so *"even at night."* Like the Psalmist, we often lie awake at night, wondering about the future. The Lord *"instructs"* even, and often, in the night watches. God had become the Counsellor, making suggestions which could gladly be followed, so the Psalmist feels compelled to praise and bless God for it. *"You have made known to me the path of life,"* *"you will fill me with joy in your presence,"* and *"eternal pleasures at your right hand,"* are all different ways of expressing the same sense of

complete satisfaction and peace focused on the eventual triumph over death itself.

1. Dear Lord, thank You for not showing me my total future *"path of life"* all at one time, but rather showing me one step at a time. Today, I especially need to be able to see:

2. In addition, Lord, I'd like to share the following with You:

We want to know the long-term
While You're showing us the short.
Help us know You see the whole
While we only see in part.

DAY TWENTY-SEVEN: CARRYING ON

CRISIS CARE: If you're a baby boomer as I am, you will remember a song from the 1970's entitled "He Ain't Heavy; He's My Brother." The lyrics go something like this:

"The road is long with many a winding turn

That leads us to who knows where, who knows where,

But I'm strong, strong enough to carry him.

He ain't heavy; he's my brother . . .

So on we go. His welfare is of my concern.

No burden is he to bear. We'll get there.

And the load doesn't weigh me down at all.

He ain't heavy; he's my brother."[1]

For those who have an adult sibling with developmental disabilities or chronic illness, these lyrics may bring mixed feelings. Research indicates that siblings are an integral part of the lives of disabled adults. At the same time, these adult siblings report that one of their greatest concerns is about the future when their parents are no longer able to provide care and support for the brother or sister with special needs, and the weight of responsibility falls on them. While adult siblings consistently report love and concern for the welfare of their disabled brother or sister, believing that "the load doesn't weigh me down at all" may be unrealistic. Trying to mesh their own personal and professional lives with the care of disabled siblings can be difficult. As a result, organizations such as the Arc (a national organization serving people with intellectual and developmental disabilities) offer support groups and educational programs for adult siblings who carry or will soon carry the full responsibility of care.²

When looking to the Bible for direction in the area of sibling care, the story of Moses comes to mind. Moses depended on his siblings many times throughout his life, so what can we learn from them? Let me suggest at least four things:

First, have a plan and work the plan. As a part of the plan to save his life, Moses' sister Miriam watched out for his safety as a baby in a basket. Miriam worked the plan so well that she even convinced Pharoah's daughter to designate Moses' mother as his nursemaid.

Second, find ways to help and to build the confidence of the disabled sibling at the same time. Brother Aaron became Moses' spokesman when Moses lacked confidence about his own eloquence, but he never took over Moses' appointed role. He did what Moses needed him to do, but he let Moses take the lead.

Third, support the sibling, but don't try to do it all alone. When victory over the Amalekites required Moses to keep his arms lifted all day, Aaron supported his arms when they became tired. Since the task was more than one person could do, Aaron had Hur to help him support Moses' arms until the victory was secure.

Finally, remember these words of wisdom I encountered recently: "Hang in there. Even Moses was once a basket case!"

CRISIS PRAYER: *"A friend loves at all times, and a brother is born for a difficult time."* (Proverbs 17:17 HCSB)

"A friend" that is a companion, *"loves at all tines"* in other words, has affection the whole way, and at any way. *"A brother is born"* meaning one is begat medically, to act as midwife, to show lineage. *"for a difficult time"* literally for *"adversity"* a

feminine noun meaning, a rival. A real friend loves his friend in prosperity and adversity. He is more than a friend in time of need - he is a brother, as one connected by the closest ties of relationship.

1. Dear Lord, thank You for providing that special person who stands with me, in brotherly kind of love, in every circumstance that I face. Today, please bless:

2. In addition, Lord, I'd like to share the following with You:

Am I my brother's keeper?
Sometimes the answer's "sure"
Andrew brought his brother;
What have you done for yours?

DAY TWENTY-EIGHT: WORKING BEHIND THE SCENES

CRISIS CARE: I enjoy the spiritual tidbits frequently found on church signs. Recently as I drove by a church near my home, I noticed these words: "Faith knows that God is working behind the scenes." As I mulled over its meaning, I found two great truths in this saying. First, I focused on the words "faith knows." They reminded me that genuine faith does not think or hope or wish or wonder. Real faith knows. The saying would carry a very different meaning if it read, "Faith hopes that God is working behind the scenes." We don't have to wish or wonder; we simply have to stand on the promises of God. As Paul wrote, *"Faith is being SURE of what we hope for and CERTAIN of what we do not see"* (Hebrews 11:1 EMPHASIS ADDED).

Second, I focused on the phrase "God is working behind the scenes." When I was in high school, I worked as stage manager for several school plays. Working backstage, I quickly realized that what the audience sees on stage is only a small part of a theatrical production. Much goes on behind the scenes to make the production come together as the director envisions it. The same is true on the stage of life. Even when we cannot see obvious manifestations of God's hand in our circumstances, He is still there and involved and working in us *"to will and to act according to his good purpose"* (Philippians 2:13). God often works in ways we cannot see!

It's comforting to know that we have a God who is working behind the scenes, when so much about caregiving also involves working behind the scenes. In writing about caregivers, gerontologist Nancy Wexler states, "You are quiet heroes, unknown except to your loved one and closest friends."[1]

Her statement is correct but incomplete. Caregivers do tend to have vast responsibilities known only to those closest to them, and most often they choose to carry out those responsibilities without compensation, recognition, or tangible reward. To complete Ms. Wexler's statement, however, two words need to be added: "You are quiet heroes, unknown except to your loved one and closest friends and God." God, who works behind the scenes in response to our faith, sees and knows and cares about every good work done in love during the private moments of caregiving.

CRISIS PRAYER: *"And if anyone gives even a cup of cold water to one of these little ones because he is my disciple, I tell you the truth, he will certainly not lose his reward."* (Matthew 10:42)

"If anyone gives" that is, causes to drink, or furnishes a drink, to the *"little ones,"* meaning little as in small physically as well as figuratively. Includes one who is small in dignity. The word was often used by rabbis in reference to their students, and as such, was a term of endearment. *"My disciple"* or pupil or learner, and this was a lesson they needed to learn, so they would not *"lose"* their *"reward,"* the word literally meaning pay, or salary or wages, but obviously meaning more as used here. Jesus would not disregard even a cup of cold water given to the humblest disciple.

1. Dear Lord, thank You for working behind the scenes and thus, demonstrating how to do that. Today, please help me as I work behind the specific scene of:

2. In addition, Lord, I'd like to share the following with You:

When we can't see You anywhere,
Give us faith to know You're there
Working in Your way and time
Instead of fitting into mine.

DAY TWENTY-NINE: CARING IN SICKNESS AND IN HEALTH

CRISIS CARE: *In sickness and in health . . . till death do us part.* Traditionally, this phrase is spoken by couples as they are joined in marriage. When life brings chronic illness or disability to one spouse, these words take on new meaning as the "well spouse" transitions into the role of caregiver.[1] While the care recipient remains a spouse, he or she may no longer be able to function as a true life partner, and the well spouse may grieve the loss of the way the relationship used to be.[2]

Many spousal caregivers report feeling "aloneness," an emotion distinctly different from loneliness. "Aloneness" is often a result of the drastic change from having a life partner with whom to enjoy everyday activities and special events, to suddenly being thrust into a position of doing things alone.[3] Others indicate they experience a loss of identity as the tasks that define the roles in a marriage change.

Decision-making is another area affected by spousal caregiving. Depending on the loved one's condition, making decisions about everyday things may change from a joint effort to an individual one. Spousal caregivers say that even more troubling are major life decisions which eventually must be made, ranging from when to move to an assisted care facility to whether to approve extensive medical procedures.

For older adults, spousal caregiving can even become a health issue for the caregiver. The Family Caregiver Alliance estimates that spousal caregivers above the age of sixty-five who are experiencing mental or emotional strain have a 63 percent higher risk of dying than non-caregivers in the same age group.[4]

So, with so many issues to deal with, how is a spousal caregiver supposed to cope? Perhaps some of the words to a song I wrote years ago for the wedding of two special friends may offer a few reminders:

> Join our lives, Father, as one.
>
> Help us hold to one another through Jesus Christ, the Son.
>
> Give us strength to bear the sorrows with the joys of our tomorrows.
>
> May we grow to love each other more each day.
>
> Join our hearts, Father, as we
>
> Pledge ourselves to one another to love eternally.
>
> Bind our hearts with understanding, and when life becomes demanding
>
> Help us turn to you for strength to find our way.
>
> Join our hands, Father, as we
>
> Take each step ahead together. We pray for unity.
>
> May we know the joy of giving; may we share the joys of living.
>
> Until hand in hand we face eternity, help us live for Thee.

CRISIS PRAYER: *"There is no fear in love. But perfect love drives out fear . . ."* (1 John 4:18)

"There is no fear" or no reason for alarm, or anxiety, or terror. The "love" spoken of is from the Greek word, agape meaning God's kind of love, as opposed to brotherly love or physical love. "Perfect love" is likewise, agape kind of love bur now referring to completeness – the kind of love that "drives out fear." John is focusing on an ideal to which Christians must aspire, but to which no one attains in this life.

1. Dear Lord, thank You for the time I had as a non-caregiver. Now, please help me as I continue to transition into the role of caregiver, especially today as I:

2. In addition, Lord, I'd like to share the following with You:

So many years you have been there
To love and cherish, honor, care.
But now it's time to lean on me.
Lord, help me be just what he needs.

DAY THIRTY: GETTING IT RIGHT

CRISIS CARE: These words were scribbled on a note pad by my nephew when he was six years old and can still be found many years later under a magnet on my refrigerator.

> Dear Vickiey
>
> I love you
>
> Zachary B.

Just learning to write and spell, Zac had an important message for me and presumably wanted to be sure it was correct. Since my first name can be and frequently is spelled several different ways (ending in i or ie or ey or y), Zac apparently wasn't sure which letters he needed, so he just used them all . . . V-i-c-k-i-e-y. In doing so, he not only gave me a treasured remembrance of his childhood, but also unknowingly illustrated an important truth: When something is really important to us, we will do as much as we can to get it right.

"Getting it right" as a caregiver can be a challenge for several reasons. First, most family caregivers have little or no training in meeting the physical and emotional needs of the care recipient. Caregivers often must actively pursue training on things as basic as proper lifting techniques to prevent injury to either party, not to mention more complex matters such as financial and legal issues. Caregivers should not hesitate to ask questions of health care providers, financial advisors, and attorneys until they have the information they need.

Another reason "getting it right" can become complicated for a caregiver is what I like to call "the changing landscape." Frequently, the conditions that create a need for caregiving in the first place may also result in inconsistency and volatility on the part of the care recipient. Involuntarily, the care recipient may perceive something as "right" one moment but "entirely wrong" the next. Keep in mind that irritating or seemingly vindictive behavior is often beyond the control of the person receiving care.

Finally, "getting it right" can be difficult when the caregiver fails to have empathy—to feel what the care recipient feels. "Try to put yourself in the patient's shoes. You will feel less angry the tenth time you are asked what day it is if you think about how it must be not to know when it is or where things are."[1]

For Jesus Christ, "getting it right" meant much more than walking in another person's shoes. Leaving the splendor of heaven, "the Word became flesh and dwelt among us." God literally became man, but He didn't stop there! Jesus lovingly and sacrificially became sin for us. *"He made the One who did not know sin to be sin for us, so that we might become the righteousness of God in Him"* (2 Corinthians 5:21 HCSB). Through His death on the cross, Jesus was able to defeat sin and death, cancel our sin debt, and become the bridge over the chasm that separated holy God and sinful humanity. Now that's what I call "getting it right"!

CRISIS PRAYER: *"To reconcile everything to Himself through Him by making peace through the blood of His cross. . . . He erased the certificate of debt, with its obligations, that was against us and opposed to us, and has taken it out of the way by nailing it to the cross."* (Colossians 1:20 and 2:14 HCSB)

"To reconcile" means to change from one state of feeling to another. Jesus didn't just reconcile some things, but *"everything."* This was done through *"the blood of His cross."* Not only did Jesus *"reconcile,"* He also *"erased,"* meaning to cancel, wash over; wipe off, wipe out, obliterate. What He *"erased"* was

our *"debt."* The fact that *"He has taken it out of the way"* is past tense, indicates that it is over. There was some allusion to a custom of cancelling documents by the striking of a nail through them. If true, this would explain the *"nailing it to the cross"* For sure, it meant the cancelled document was now publicized on the cross so that all might read it.

1. Dear Lord, thank You for reconciling everything to Yourself, and erasing my debt, thus allowing me to get it right. Help me today, especially as I try to:

2. In addition, Lord, I'd like to share the following with You:

> *I used to try with all my might*
> *To follow rules, to do what's right.*
> *But now I know that I am free*
> *Because You paid it all for me.*

DAY THIRTY-ONE: CONTROLLING WORRY AND ANXIETY

CRISIS CARE: Most likely, you are familiar with the *Serenity Prayer*, written by American theologian Reinhold Niebuhr:

God grant me the serenity to accept the things I cannot change,

The courage to change the things I can,

And the wisdom to know the difference.

This prayer reminds us of the futility of worry. In essence, he tells us that it is useless to worry about things we *can* change. Rather than worrying, we should use our energy and time to accomplish change. In like manner, it makes no sense to worry about things we *cannot* change because no matter how much we worry, they're not going to change. Instead, we should channel our efforts in a more positive and productive direction.

In caregiving, issues arise over which we have no control, but about which much time and energy can be wasted by worrying. Often, these are "how long" questions: How long will I have my loved one with me? How long will our finances hold out? How long will I hold out? How long will my loved one remember me? How long until the condition worsens? While worries and fears are normal in caregiving, excessive anxiety can interfere with daily functioning and can even cause physical symptoms such as headaches, stomach upsets, rapid breathing, fast heart rate, trembling, and irritability.

"The key to managing anxiety is to find the balance between reality, fears, and worries. Stay focused on this balance, and do not give in to excessive negative thoughts," psychologist Dr. Shachi Shantinath tells caregivers. "Pay attention to your breathing when you feel anxious or fearful. Take deep, full, and slow breaths and that will help to return a sense of calm." Additionally, prayer and meditation are effective ways to still the mind when worries are rampant.[1]

Before Niebuhr and before Dr. Shantinath, the apostle Paul identified the importance of prayer in controlling anxiety. In Philippians 4:6, Paul suggests that we replace our anxieties with prayer, our worries with thanksgiving, and our uncertainties with requests to God. Remember, life's worries will never knock you for a loop when you are leaning on the everlasting arms.

CRISIS PRAYER: *"Do not be anxious about anything, but in everything, by prayer, and petition, with thanksgiving, present your requests to God."* (Philippians 4:6)

The word for *"anxious"* means distracted. We who are so easily distracted by worries, should take *"everything"* to God in prayer and *"present"* them to Him, that is make them known to Him. Painful anxiety is inevitable to those who feel alone in mere self-dependence with the difficulties and dangers of life. So we pray.

"Pray" (a word meaning general worship), *"petition,"* (which includes supplication – prayer for self and for things, and in this case, probably includes intercession, which is prayer for others), and *"thanksgiving"* (which is the natural accompaniment for prayer requests), are meant to summarize the totality of our communication with God.

1. Dear Lord, thank You for allowing me to present my anxieties to You through prayer. Today, I especially prayer for:

2. In addition, Lord, I'd like to share the following with You:

We are so prone to worry, Lord,
Instead of trusting in your Word.
The things we cannot change You can,
When we just place them in your hands.

DAY THIRTY-TWO: CARING FOR THE TERMINALLY ILL

CRISIS CARE: Today I want to share with you a poem written by a friend of mine for her stepmother, who was the caregiver for her terminally ill father. I believe my friend, Sandra Winner, does a marvelous job of capturing the struggles and commitments of "The Caregiver's World."

I am watching the world, people rushing to and fro
Their minds are on their duties
My mind is full of memories

I used to be like them, one day I'll join their rank
But today I'm on the outside, living with the dying
Consumed with the struggling of another

Once he was strong like I am, but now he is frail
each day seems slow with forced routine
but our trip is almost through as I watch him quickly fail

I want to spend it wisely, this time will not last
Savoring each stolen quiet moment
Reminiscing, reliving, and sharing the past

It's hard to be where I am, My heart is filled with grief

So many questions to be answered
But for him it's like relief

Do you see me as you hurry to and fro
Only the facade you want to see
I am beside you but not with you. Do you see me?

I long to join you from this place
I will not leave the struggles he must face
He brought me here through your rushing world
Now he needs my tending
to bring him through this time of ending

Someday I will not be consumed by him,
My world returned to me
But I will have my memories
of this time of ending and his time of strength.[1]

CRISIS PRAYER: *"Entreat me not to leave thee, or to return from following after thee: for whither thou goest, I will go; and where thou lodgest, I will lodge; thy people shall be my people, and thy God my God. Where thou diest, will I die, and there will I be buried: the Lord do so to me, and more also, if ought but death part me and thee."* (Ruth 1:16–17 KJV)

Ruth's mind was made up. She would not be wrenched away from her mother-in-law. The length of the journey, its dangers, and the inevitable fatigue accompanying it, did not hinder her resolution. Had not her mother-in-law the same distance to travel, the same fatigue to endure, the same perils to encounter? Might not the aged traveler, derive some assistance and cheer from the company of a young, willing companion? Ruth was resolved. Nothing on earth would separate them. "Where thou lodgest" is not a reference to the ultimate destination, but to the nightly stops, coming from the verb meaning to tarry all night. *"Thy people shall be my people, and thy God my God."* There being no verb in the original language, we might assume Ruth was claiming, Naomi's people and Naomi's God were already her own.

1. Dear Lord, thank You for demonstrating for me the steadfast endurance of Ruth. May I display similar characteristics today toward the one for whom I am giving care. I especially prayer for:

2. In addition, Lord, I'd like to share the following with You:

Lord, we know the end is near.
I know it; so does he.
Help us to face it without fear,
For we are safe in Thee.

DAY THIRTY-THREE: LEARNING LESSONS FROM A CAT

CRISIS CARE: If you are a cat person, you will undoubtedly relate to these caregiving lessons from the cat! If you're not a cat person, the following provide a good summary of key points from previous devotionals. Either way, here are some words of wisdom and advice from our furry friends:[1]

(1) *Take a happy nap on the couch.* Caregiving can be exhausting, so catch a little down time whenever you can.

(2) *Get petted as often as possible.* Caregivers need regular breaks from their routine responsibilities. Find ways to pamper yourself occasionally.

(3) *Land on your feet every time you fall.* Caregivers should seek to maintain balance in their lives. With balance, every small slip won't turn your world upside down.

(4) *Be aware when something's fishy.* Unfortunately, caregivers and their care recipients, especially senior adults, can be easy prey for dishonesty and scams. The old saying is true: If it seems too good to be true, it probably is!

(5) *Stay on top of things.* Caregiving usually comes with medical, business, and financial issues to be handled. Don't procrastinate or ignore them.

(6) *Don't dig in the litter for very long.* Almost everyone experiences negative thoughts and self-pity at times, but don't allow yourself to dwell in them.

(7) *When you have a fur ball, cough it up.* Holding feelings and emotions inside can be unhealthy, both physically and emotionally. Let them out by sharing with a friend or support group.

(8) *Curiosity never killed anything except a little time.* Don't hesitate to ask lots of questions to those who help with medical, financial, and legal issues.

(9) *You can only stretch so far.* Be careful not to stretch yourself too thin. Be aware of when you are reaching your limits, and ask for help.

(10) *Scratch when it itches.* Taking care of your own needs as well as those of the care recipient will help prevent burnout.

(11) *Get someone else to clean your bathroom.* As a caregiver, don't try to go it alone. Ask others for assistance with everyday tasks while you carry out your caregiving responsibilities.

(12) *Always rest in the sun ...* or in our case, the Son. In the midst of all the activities and responsibilities that accompany caregiving, find your rest in the Son, who issues this invitation: *"Come to me, all you who are weary and burdened, and I will give you rest."* (Matthew 11:28)

CRISIS PRAYER: *"But ask the animals, and they will teach you, or the birds of the air, and they will tell you; or speak to the earth, and it will teach you, or let the fish of the sea inform you. Which of all these does not know that the hand of the Lord has done this? In His hand is the life of every creature and the breath of all mankind."* (Job 12:7–10)

Job here begins his review of all creation, to show that God has the absolute direction of it, and if appeals were made to the animals, and they were asked their position with respect to God, they would with one voice proclaim Him their Creator and Provider. *"Speak to the earth"* includes its orderly course, its summers and winters, its seedtime and harvest, its former and latter rains, its constant productivity, which, no less than animal instincts, speak of a single ruling power directing and ordering all things. *'The breadth of all mankind"* completes the list of all those who are wholly dependent on Him.

1. Dear Lord, thank You for teaching me lessons from every relationship of my life. Today, I especially could learn from:

2. In addition, Lord, I'd like to share the following with You:

*Teach me lessons everyday
From everything that comes my way.
Creation shows Your power, Lord,
In ways too mighty to ignore.*

DAY THIRTY-FOUR: RELATING TO OTHERS

CRISIS CARE: Whether we like to admit it or not, caregiving can impact not only the relationship between caregiver and care recipient, but also other relationships with family, friends, and co-workers. For instance, family members who see the loved one infrequently may think the caregiver exaggerates the extent of care needed. Out-of-town siblings may become critical of the care being given, question decisions made by the caregiver, or experience feelings of guilt for not being able to help more. These reactions can then cause the caregiver to feel resentful or unappreciated, resulting in strained family relationships.[1]

Friendships can also bear the brunt of caregiving stress. As mentioned previously, caregivers have a tendency to isolate themselves from friends and social situations for many reasons, not the least of which is lack of time and energy. Additionally, caregivers for those whose functioning has changed because of severe illness or injury report that friends sometimes seem uncomfortable with the new situation and, after the initial outpouring of concern, tend to drift away.[2]

In the work arena, caregiving responsibilities may affect the employer/employee relationship in a negative manner. "Employers might not recognize that they have an employee who comes to their job and works a full eight- or ten-hour day; then that same employee leaves work to go care for an elderly parent or loved one," says Brad Hancock of Paragon Senior Care. "Their day may not end until very late at night." While employers and co-workers are generally understanding of childcare problems, they may not understand eldercare needs.

According to the National Family Caregivers Association, however, eldercare is projected to replace childcare as the number one dependent care issue in the United States by 2005.[3]

So, what's a Christian caregiver to do in the face of potential relationship problems such as these? Consider the advice of the apostle Paul:

"Don't have anything to do with foolish and stupid arguments, because you know they produce quarrels. And the Lord's servant must not quarrel; instead he must be kind to everyone, able to teach, not resentful" (2 Timothy 2:23–24).

"And I want you to stress these things, so that those who have trusted in God may be careful to devote themselves to doing what is good. These things are excellent and profitable to everyone. But avoid foolish controversies and genealogies and arguments and quarrels . . . because these are unprofitable and useless" (Titus 2:8–9).

"Bear with one another and forgive whatever grievances you may have against one another. Forgive as the Lord forgave you. And over all these virtues put on love, which binds them all together in perfect unity" (Colossians 3:13–14).

"Live in harmony with one another. Do not be proud . . . . If it is possible, as far as it depends on you, live at peace with everyone. Do not be overcome by evil, but overcome evil with good" (Romans 12:16–18, 21).

Enough said!

CRISIS PRAYER: *"Whatever happens, conduct yourselves in a manner worthy of the gospel of Christ."* (Philippians 1:27a)

"Conduct yourselves" means to live life as a good citizen. Paul exhorts the Philippians to boldness and steadfastness, under possible conflict or even under persecution which threatened them. Only here in Paul's writings, the verb means to be a

citizen, a citizen worthily of the Gospel. *"Worthy of the gospel"* is an adverb from the Greek word *axios*, meaning appropriately. Those who profess to be Christians, should live as though they believe gospel truths, submit to gospel laws, and depend upon gospel promises.

1. Dear Lord, thank You for family, friends and associates who care, but who may have negative impressions of what I do as a caregiver. Please help me to be patient with them. Today, I especially pray for by relationship with:

2. In addition, Lord, I'd like to share the following with You:

Help us avoid the petty things
And quarrels they so easily bring.
Rather to live peaceably,
We look to you for unity.

DAY THIRTY-FIVE: MOVING BEYOND GOOD INTENTIONS

CRISIS CARE: Caregiving can be filled with good intentions: I'm going to be more patient with the one I'm caring for. I'm going to take better care of myself. I'm going to stop putting off that decision. I'm going to find time to start going to that support group. I'm going to ask ____ for a little help with ____. (You fill in the blanks!) While it's important to make those kinds of decisions, moving beyond good intentions requires more than just deciding.

In his Christian counseling seminars, my brother adapts the story of six little frogs sitting on a log. One of the frogs says, "I'm going to jump off this log!" My brother then asks, "How many frogs are left on the log?" Most of the time the seminar participants respond, "Five." "No," my brother retorts, "there are still six, because the first frog never really got around to jumping!" His point, of course, is that deciding to do something, or even talking about doing something, is different than actually doing it.[1]

We human beings are experts at having good intentions. How many of us made New Year's resolutions this year, just to break them before February? How many diets or exercise programs have we begun, only to fall off the wagon? How many times have we said, "I'm going to get my taxes done early this year," and then find ourselves filling out tax forms at midnight on April 14? How many of you have read something in this book, decided to make a change, and like the little frog on the log, just haven't gotten around to it?

In Philippians, Paul says that God works in us *"to will and to do."* To will (deciding) is followed by to do (taking action).

Choosing to take action on a decision is what moves us beyond good intentions. Perhaps Nike has the right idea when their ads encourage us, "Just Do It!"

As we near the end of Forty Days of Care, my prayer is that something you have read has triggered ideas about things you need to do or perhaps stop doing. More important than reading anything written in these pages, however, will be asking the same question Saul asked when he encountered Christ on the road to Damascus: *"Lord, what wilt thou have me to do?"* (Acts 22:10 KJV).

Ask yourself that question, listen for His answer, and then . . .

CRISIS PRAYER: *". . . do it, not only when their eye is on you and to win their favor, but with sincerity of heart and reverence for the Lord. Whatever you do, work at it with all your heart, as working for the Lord, not for men."* (Colossians 3:22–23)

"Do it with . . . sincerity of heart" is from the Greek word meaning simplicity, purity, graciousness, *"and reverence"* meaning in awe of. What we do is to be motivated by inward principle, not by outward compulsion, *"with all your heart"* better translated, with all your being. You are *"working for the Lord"* from the Greek word *kuros*, meaning master, supreme in authority. Every difficult and challenging task is dignified by the thought of it being done for the Lord, and *"not for men."*

1. Dear Lord, thank You for allowing me to make decisions that are for You and not for others. Today, I pray that you will help me to do what I decide to do, especially:

2. In addition, Lord, I'd like to share the following with You:

Lord, You know I mean well when
I just resolve to do again
The things I've meant to do before . . .
Remind me who I'm working for.

DAY THIRTY-SIX: LOOKING UP

CRISIS CARE: Have you noticed that, to a great extent, we are becoming a society that looks down? With smart phones, smart watches, fitness trackers, and tablets, we often tend to walk and ride (but hopefully not drive!) with our heads down, looking at the technology that has become such a huge part of our lives. Some suggest that in doing so, we are missing the people, the places, the important things of life around us. In his poem "Look Up," Gary Turk expresses it this way:

So look up from your phone, shut down display.

Take in your surroundings, make the most of today.

Just one real connection is all it can take,

to show you the difference that being there can make.[1]

While there's no doubt that smartphones and other technology have made life easier by affording many conveniences and instant access to the world, therapist Jonathan Alpert suggests that we need to "learn how to outsmart your smartphone so it doesn't prevent you from enjoying the richness of life." We need to find ways to strike a balance between smartphone use and smartphone reliance, he says, and look-up from our devices more.[2]

We tend to make the same mistake with our emotional and spiritual needs. Whether coping with loneliness, emptiness, grief, guilt, or the many other feelings we encounter, we often fail to "look up" in two important ways. First, we need to look up to see those around us. I truly believe that God provides friends, pastors, counselors, support groups and others to help us through the hard times, often serving as an extension of God's hands in the world. Second, and most importantly, we need to "look up" to God in the same sense as the psalmist when he wrote, *"I will lift up my eyes to the hills—where does my help come from? My help comes from the Lord, the Maker of heaven and earth"* (Psalm 121:1–2).

Consider an instance when Jesus looked up: *"... and **looking up** to heaven, he blessed, and brake, and gave the loaves to his disciples, and the disciples to the multitude"* (Matthew 14:19b KJV, EMPHASIS ADDED). Each of His actions in this verse has its own significance: *Looking up to heaven,* Jesus was acknowledging the Source of His power and provision. When *He blessed,* he demonstrated His reliance on the power of prayer. As *He brake* and *gave,* Jesus acted upon His prayer with faith. Finally, *He gave the loaves to his disciples and the disciples to the multitude,* depending on His followers as extensions of Himself to meet the needs of those who needed to be nourished and restored.

For caregivers, unresolved emotions can easily lead to burnout. Gerontologist Nancy Wexler states, "It is entirely understandable and human that any person who shoulders full responsibility for another should burn out. Caring for someone who cannot survive without you is both emotionally and physically draining, no matter how much you may love the person."[3] So, when you are feeling especially human and when burnout is smoldering just below the surface, LOOK UP. Restoration comes when we look up, acknowledge the Source of our strength, rely on the power of prayer, act upon our prayers in faith, and depend upon those God chooses to use as channels of His blessings in our lives.

CRISIS PRAYER: *"I will lift up my eyes to the hills—where does my help come from? My help comes from the Lord, the Maker of heaven and earth"* (Psalm 121:1–2)

"To the hills" is the direction to which the Psalmist lifted his eyes, and in so doing, he was prompted to ask a question, "where does my help come from?" Being a Psalm of Accent, the "hills" are those on which Jerusalem is built, thus increasing the need for the question. Possibly, the Psalmist may in his mind have been contrasting the confidence with which a worshipper of God might look up to the sacred city on the crest of the holy hill as if there and there alone was his help. Given this possibility, the question becomes even more important. The answer to his questions was, "My help comes from the Lord," not from the superstition of the Canaanites, that help would come from the sacred heights of the holy city, but from its "Maker," who alone had the power to help.

1. Dear Lord, thank that my help comes from You, and that You are always available, if I will just look for You. Today, I pray that I will be able to see You especially in:

2. In addition, Lord, I'd like to share the following with You:

We lift our eyes to You, our God,
For strength to walk each path we trod.
And when we feel we can't do more,
We look to You to be restored.

DAY THIRTY-SEVEN: OVERCOMING OBSTACLES

CRISIS CARE: Encountering and overcoming obstacles is a part of every aspect of our lives, and caregiving is no exception. In addition to medical and financial obstacles related to the loved one's condition, caregiving may also build walls of isolation, relationship problems, family stress, and emotional strain. Overcoming these kinds of obstacles is extremely important, but often difficult.

Joshua and the Israelites faced a huge obstacle soon after crossing the Jordan River to enter the Promised Land. Their obstacle, of course, was the wall around Jericho. We all know the story . . . if not from the Scriptures, then from the old spiritual song. And we know what happens: "Joshua fought the battle of Jericho, and the walls came tumbling down!" As we seek to overcome our own obstacles, perhaps we can learn a few strategies from Joshua:

(1) Recognize the power and holiness of God. Before Joshua received God's message about Jericho, he was told to remove his sandals because he was on holy ground. He did so without hesitation.

(2) Listen to the Lord's instructions and follow them. God's plan for overcoming the obstacle at Jericho may have seemed a little strange to Joshua, but he followed it exactly as he was told.

(3) Rely on the spiritual leaders God has placed in your life. After receiving God's directions, Joshua relayed the message to the Israelites. When Joshua had spoken to the people, he ordered them, "Advance!" and they did.

(4) Trust the Lord's timing. God commanded Joshua and the army of Israel to march around the city of Jericho for six days

and then on the seventh day to march around it seven times. Only then was God ready to give them the city. Acting too quickly or waiting too long undoubtedly would have brought disaster.

(5) Remember God can provide a way out in the midst of chaos. Inside Jericho, Rahab and her family seemed destined for annihilation as were the other residents of the city. However, God—and therefore Joshua—did not forget her.

(6) Give the Lord what belongs to Him. Joshua told his soldiers, *"All the silver and gold and the articles of bronze and iron are sacred to the Lord and must go into his treasury."* (Joshua 6:19)

(7) Believe that God can overcome obstacles that seem insurmountable. Facing a massive walled city that was "tightly shut up," Joshua and the Israelites believed the word of the Lord . . . and the walls came tumbling down."

CRISIS PRAYER: *"The seventh time around, when the priests sounded the trumpet blast, Joshua commanded the people, 'Shout! For the Lord has given you the city!' . . . and at the sound of the trumpet, when the people gave a loud shout, the wall collapsed . . ."* (Joshua 6:16, 20)

"Joshua commanded the people, 'Shout'!" This was not just a loud yell. The word means to split the ears, in order to strike fear in their enemies. In this case, the people needed to shout loud enough to be heard over the sound of the trumpets. It worked! *"When the people gave a loud shout, the wall collapsed."* No hand of man caused this catastrophe, no natural causes brought about the fall. The fall was a result of the faith of God's people. Hebrews 11:30 says, *"By faith, the walls of Jericho fell down."*

1. Dear Lord, thank You for equipping me with enough faith to overcome all obstacles that come my way. I especially need Your help today as I :

2. In addition, Lord, I'd like to share the following with You:

Facing walls and obstacles
We cannot climb alone,
We lift our voices up to You,
For You can bring them down.

DAY THIRTY-EIGHT: IMPROVING AS A CAREGIVER

CRISIS CARE: As I worked on this project, I kept several folders on my computer desktop for devotionals in various stages of completion. I had entitled one folder "caregiver in progress" for pieces I had just started or ideas for new ones. I looked at that folder many, many times before I realized that's what I was . . . a caregiver in progress. Do you remember the children's song, "He's Still Working on Me" or the bumper sticker that read, "Be patient, God's not finished with me yet"? That's me as a caregiver! As I researched and wrote these daily readings, I often found myself thinking, "Do as I say, not as I do," knowing I still had a long way to go before I was really following my own advice. But that's okay, because caregiving—like child rearing—doesn't come with instructions . . . or does it?

Thankfully, there are many resources available to those who need help or information. These are a few of the numerous books available:

- *And Thou Shalt Honor: The Caregiver's Companion* (McLeod, ed.)
- *The Comfort of Home: An Illustrated Step-by-Step Guide* (Meyer)
- *The Complete Guide To Eldercare* (Jones-Lee and Callender)
- *The Fearless Caregiver* (Barg)
- *Fourteen Friends Guide to Eldercaring* (Cooper, ed.)

- *The Gift of Caregiving* (Goldman)
- *How To Care for Aging Parents: A Complete Guide* (Morris)
- *I'll Take Care of You* (Ilardo and Rothman)

Additionally, the "dot.com" world provides a plethora of information sources on the internet. Here are just a few:

www.aarp.org/caregiving

www.caregiving.org

www.caregiver.com

www.eldercare.acl.gov

www.caregiver.org

www.nfcacares.org

www.caregiving.com

www.nia.nih.go

All of these are great resources, but none can compare to the best instruction book of all—the Holy Bible. In its pages, God has given us the instruction book for every aspect of life. As I hope I've demonstrated in these readings, all the joys, sorrows, rewards, and frustrations of caregiving are addressed more than adequately in the Scriptures. His Word gives us instructions on how to mature as Christians and how to develop Christlike character. As Rick Warren reminds us, "There is only one way to develop the habits of Christlike character: You must *practice* them— and that takes time! *There are no instant habits.* Paul urged Timothy, *'Practice these things. Devote your life to them so that everyone can see your progress'*" (1 Timothy 4:15 GWT).[1] As we allow the Holy Spirit to produce the fruit of love, joy, peace, patience, gentleness, goodness, meekness, self-control and faith in our lives, and as we practice Christlike character daily, we can improve not only in our caregiving, but in all we do.

CRISIS PRAYER: *"Being confident of this, that he who began a good work in you will carry it on to completion until the day of Christ Jesus"* (Philippians 1:6)

The *"good work"* is God's; He began it and He will perfect it. God who works in you, will *"carry it on to completion"* that is, He will complete, accomplish, and perfect that which He has begun in you. In Paul's view, God's grace is the beginning and the end; our co-operation lies in the intermediate process linking both together. This is made still plainer in the next chapter of Philippians. Paul does not define *"the day of Christ Jesus"* as being either near or far away, he only declares that God is still at work. To the individual believer that *"day"* is practically the day of his death.

1. Dear Lord, thank You that You are not through with me yet, nor will you ever be, until my life is over. I especially need You to work in me today as I:

2. In addition, Lord, I'd like to share the following with You:

> *I know I'm not all I should be*
> *Or everything You want for me.*
> *Lord, make me just a ball of clay*
> *So you can mold me in Your Way.*

DAY THIRTY-NINE: SAYING GOODBYE

CRISIS CARE: If the Lord tarries, most of us will come to the point of saying goodbye to the loved one for whom we have provided care and support. For some, the journey to that place will be long and difficult. Others will feel helpless as the time speeds by uncontrollably fast. How should we approach the process of saying goodbye? The answer was brought into focus for me by an article in Baylor Magazine, which I cut out and hung near my mirror so that I would see it every day.

In the article, Dr. Lauren Barron, a physician in private practice in Waco, Texas, tells of a lesson she learned while in medical school. A lecturer on Alzheimer's explained to the med students that he and his wife cared for a dear relative who could not walk, talk, bathe, or clothe herself. She was in diapers and required constant supervision, yet the speaker spoke with delight of the pleasure and privilege of caring for her. Then he revealed he was talking about their infant daughter, not an elderly relative as the students assumed.

"I never have forgotten his point about how gladly we care for our babies—how tenderly and lovingly and with what joy and hope. But the same care required by our elders, we give grudgingly, with pity or dread and with a sense of futility, tragedy, and grief," Dr. Barron states. "He challenged us to approach the care of the elderly, whether as physicians or family members, with more hope, more optimism, more joy and more of a sense of privilege—to say goodbye as well as we say hello."[1]

As caregivers, we do not control when or where we will say goodbye to our loved one. What we can control is how—our attitudes and actions during the process of saying goodbye. Whether that process is long or short, it matters how we treat those whose care God has entrusted to us. It matters that we say goodbye with love and kindness and, yes, even with joy.

CRISIS PRAYER: *"And this is my prayer: that your love may abound more and more in knowledge and depth of insight so that you may be able to discern what is best . . ."* (Philippians 1:9–10a)

The *"prayer"* is about God's *"love"* and the Greek word is *agape.* In Paul's day, the language had several words for *"love"* reflecting whether the *"love"* was for a brother, a fellow believer, or whether the *"love"* was of a physical nature, or whether the *"love"* was God's kind of *"love,"* the Greek word being *agape.* Here, Paul is referring to God's kind of *"love,"* and that it would *"abound,"* that is to be in excess, to be superfluous. Paul prays that God's love would *"abound . . . in knowledge"* that is discernment, and recognition, as well as in *"insight"* that would enable us to *"discern what is best,"* that is, what is excellent.

1. Dear Lord, only You know when the last moments will be in the life of a loved one. May I continue to reflect Your excellent love until that final moment. But today, Lord, help me especially to:

2. In addition, Lord, I'd like to share the following with You:

Lord, you know that we will cry
When it's time to say goodbye,

But may we trust our last farewell
Means they're home with You to dwell.

DAY FORTY: SAYING HELLO AGAIN

CRISIS CARE: As I write today, little signs of spring have begun to show themselves. Trees are beginning to bud; flowers are starting to blossom; birds are singing happily in the backyard. All around me the things that looked so desolate during the dead of winter show signs of new life. In all of nature, spring reminds us that death is not the end. On the contrary, it is the beginning of new life. For Christians, death is *"to be absent from the body and to be present with Christ,"* who guides us as we take our next step into eternity (2 Corinthians 5:8 KJV).

Caregiving often ends with the care recipient making the transition from the arms of the caregiver into the arms of the Lord. While saying goodbye will naturally bring sorrow, we as Christians can be comforted in the fact that our goodbyes are not forever.

As we complete our forty days together, I want to leave you with several thoughts of comfort and assurance. Whether your goodbyes are close at hand, far into the future, or already spoken, the Lord wants to remind you that you will be saying "hello" again!

First, Jesus has already won the victory over death. *"Death has been swallowed up in victory. O death, where is thy sting? O grave, where is thy victory? . . . But thanks be to God, which giveth us the victory through our Lord Jesus Christ"* (1 Corinthians 15:54–55, 57 KJV).

Next, Jesus promised He is preparing a place for us. *"In my Father's house are many rooms; if it were not so, I would have told you. I am going there to prepare a place for you. And if I go and prepare a place for you, I will come back and take you with me that you also may be where I am"* (John 14:2–3).

In the meantime, Jesus leaves for us a supernatural peace. *"Peace I leave with you; my peace I give you. I do not give to you as the world gives. Do not let your hearts be troubled, and do not be afraid"* (John 14:27).

Finally, as Christians we will experience the eternal joys of heaven together. *"And God shall wipe away every tear from their eyes; there shall be no more death, nor sorrow, nor crying. There shall be no more pain, for the former things have passed away"* (Revelation 21:4 KJV).

CRISIS PRAYER: *". . . and so shall we ever be with the Lord. Wherefore, comfort one another with these words."* (1 Thessalonians 4:17–18 KJV)

"And so . . ." Paul has forever settled the difference between the dead and the living, and he does not think it necessary to describe what is immediately to follow, since the Thessalonians were sure to know. It only remained for him to say that having once joined with the Lord, they would never be parted from Him, but would share a blessed eternity participating with His glory. Paul does not choose to describe judgment because his object was to *"comfort"* the Thessalonians in their bereavement. The word *"comfort"* means to encourage and literally means to call another person near to you for the purpose of sharing encouraging words with them.

1. Dear Lord, thank You that the end is not the end. I take comfort in that fact. Thank You for allowing me to be a

caregiver. As I reflect on my days of caregiving, I give thanks especially for:

2. In addition, Lord, I'd like to share the following with You:

*Thank you for these words to share
With others as we seek to care.
Our joys and tears we'll bring to You
Until You have made all things new.
Amen.*

APPENDIX A
CAREGIVER'S SELF-RATING SCALE*

1. Abandonment—To withdraw protection or support or to actively abuse your care-receiver.

2. Neglect—To allow life-threatening situations to persist or to display consistent coldness or anger.

3. Detachment/aloofness—To maintain an air of detachment or being aloof, perfunctory in your care, no genuine concern, only obligation. Concerned only with the physical well-being of your care-receiver.

4. General support—Given freely, with a guarded degree of warmth and respect, occasional feeling of manipulation. Concerned with both emotional and physical well-being of care-receiver.

5. Express empathy—the ability to feel what your care-receiver feels, a quality relationship where feeling can be freely expressed and caringly received with non-judgmental positive regard.

6. Sympathy—Feeling sorry for the care-receiver, giving sympathy, focusing on the losses experienced by care-receiver.

7. Occasional over-involvement—Care characterized by periodic attempts to do for rather than be with.

8. Consistent over-involvement—Care-receiver regarded as object of series of tasks which must be performed.

9. Heroic over-involvement—Care characterized by sometimes frantic and desperate attempts to provide for every possible

need your care-receiver has; increased dependence, care-receiver not allowed independence.

10. Fusion of personalities—Between caregiver and care-receiver. The caregiver's needs no longer have any value or meaning; the caregiver has abandoned herself to needs of the care-receiver.

*Used by permission from the San Diego Mental Health Services

END NOTES

WHY A BOOK FOR CAREGIVERS?

1. "Caregiver Statistics." Caregiver Action Network Website. https://caregiveraction.org/resources/caregiver-statistics, pp. 1–6.

2. Libert, Anne Blanford. "Elderly Parents and Adult Children as Caregivers. Highlights: An ERIC/CAPS Digest." ERIC Clearinghouse on Counseling and Personnel Services. ERIC Identifier: ED279993, p. 1.

3. "Caregiver Statistics: Demographics." Family Caregiver Alliance Website. https://www.caregiver.org/caregiver-statistics-demographics, p. 1.

4. "The Grandparenting Generation." New Republic Magazine Website. https://newrepublic.com/article/146519/grandparenting-generation, pp.1-2.

5. "Taking Care of Others: Caregiving." Erie County Department of Senior Services Website. www.erie.gov/depts/seniorservices/taking_care_of_others.phtml, p. 1.

6. "What Is Caregiving and Who Are America's Caregivers." National Family Caregivers Association Website, 2004. www.nfcacares.org, p. 1.

7. Warren, Rick. *The Purpose-Driven Life*. Grand Rapids, Michigan: Zondervan, 2002, pp. 9–10.

THE ROLE OF PRAYER IN A TIME OF CRISIS

1. Unless otherwise noted, all scripture in this chapter is from *The Holy Bible: The New King James Version*, copyright 1979, 1980, 1982, 1988 by Thomas Nelson, Inc. Publishers. All rights reserved.

DAY ONE

1. "New Caregivers in Crisis: Getting Back Control of Your Life." AgingCare Website. www.agingcare.com/Articles/new-caregiver-crisis-155471.htm. p. 1.

2. "'Consuming and Isolating': Why the Caregiver Crisis Could Strain Public Health Care." Courier News and Home News Tribune. https://www.mycentraljersey.com/indepth/news/local/outreach/2019/01/23/caregivers-crisis-private-public-health-care-challenge-nj/2451423002/, p.1.

3. Berinato, Scott. "That Discomfort You're Feeling Is Grief." Harvard Business Review. https://hbr.org/2020/03/that-discomfort-youre-feeling-is-grief?fbclid=IwAR1U5fQAQ7B7xeluef8HOKH43cEoiiGmrMQh4wicgAYgiOoB7ePc8aRmTPs. March 23, 2020.

4. Warren, Rick. "5 Biblical Principles When Facing a Devastating Crisis." Pastors.com Website. https://pastors.com/5-biblical-principles-when-facing-a-devastating-crisis/, September 16, 2017.

Day Two

1. "Brain Attack: The Family's Role in Caregiving." Dallas: American Heart Association Brochure, p. 22.
2. "Elder Care." PacifiCare Behavioral Health, Inc. Website. , www.pbhi.com/members_public/memyfamily/eldercare, p. 1.
3. "Caregiving: Managing Stress When Giving Care." AARP Webplace. www.aarp.org/confacts/caregive/mngstress, pp. 1–5

Day Four

1. "Taking Care of Others," p.1.
2. Calkin, Ruth Harms. Tell Me Again, Lord, I Forget. Colorado Springs, Colorado: David C. Cook Publishing Company, 1974

Day Five

1. Taylor Gifts Catalog 2003, p. 63.
2. "10 Timely Tips for Caregivers." Senior Health Care Website. www.senior-health-care.com/tips-for-caregivers.htm, p. 1.
1. "The Importance of Touch." Aribella Magazine Website. www.aribella.com/touch.htm, p. 1.
2. "10 Timely Tips," p. 2.

Day Six

1. Angelou, Maya. Hallmark's Maya Angelou Life Mosaic Collection. © 2003 Maya Angelou. Used by permission.

Day Seven

2. Crawford, Dan R. DiscipleShape: Twelve Weeks to Spiritual Fitness. Peabody, MA: Hendrickson Publishers, 1998, pp. 94–96.
3. "Alzheimer's Disease: What it is . . . What We're Doing About It!" Alzheimer's Disease and Related Disorders Association Pamphlet, 2003, p.
4. Crawford, p. 96.

Day Eight

1. Sweat, Rebecca. "How Pets Help Senior Citizens." PetPlace.com Website. www.petplace.netscape.com/articles, p. 1.
2. "The Healing Power of Pets." Pets and Senior Citizens Website. www.seniors-site.com/petsm/needpets, pp. 1–2.
3. Wohlberg, Steve. Will My Pet Go To Heaven? Enumclaw, WA: WinePress Publishing, 2002.

Day Nine

1. "Caregiving: Managing Stress," p. 3.

2. Hunt, Dee Dee. "Caregiving." Scleroderma from A to Z. The International Scleroderma Network Website. www.sclero.org/support/caregivers/dee-dee, p. 3.

3. Brown, Denise M. "Focus on You: Tips for Caregivers." Caregiving Newsletter Online Support August 1997, www.caregiving.com/support, p. 4.

4. From "Love Is Something You Do" by David Baker © 1969 Hope Publishing Co., Carol Stream, IL. All right reserved. Used by permission.

5. "Christians, Anger, and Forgiveness." Walking Wounded.Net Website. www.walking-wounded.net/html/anger.html, pp. 4–5.

Day Eleven

1. "UK: Care of the Elderly Often Lacks Dignity." Global Action on Aging Website. www.globalaging.org/health/world/dignity, May 28, 2003, p. 1.

Day Twelve

2. Wooten, Patty. "Laughter as Therapy for Patient and Caregiver." Pulmonary

3. Rehabilitation, ed. Hodgkin. Philadelphia: Lippincott, 1993.

4. "Caring for the Caregiver." The Caregiver's Handbook. San Diego County Mental Health Services. www.acsu.buffalo.edu/~drstall/hndbk0.html.

Day Thirteen

1. Pfeiffer, Beverly. "Myths About the Aging Process." Work and Family Life

2. Newsletter, October, 1993, University of Missouri Outreach and Extension. Available online at www.outreach.missouri.edu/cmregion/thriving.

3. Abel, Barbara. "With Alzheimer's, the Caregiver Is a Patient, Too." Healthlink. Medical College of Wisconsin, 2003. Available online at healthlink.mcw.edu/article/1031002313.

4. Neukrug, Linda. "October 27 Devotional." Daily Guideposts 2001. Carmel, NY: Guidepost, p. 314.

Day Fourteen

1. "Alzheimer's Disease/Senility." Calgary Health Region Website. www.calgaryhealthregion.ca/hlthconn/items/alz.htm, p. 2.

Day Fifteen

1. "In the Middle: A Report on Multicultural Boomers Coping with Family and Aging Issues." American Association of Retired Persons (AARP) Website. www.aarp.org/inthemiddle, pp. 1-2.

Day Sixteen

1. "Alzheimer's Disease: What It Is ... What We're Doing About It!" Alzheimer's Disease and Related Disorders Association Pamphlet, 2003, p. 4.

Day Seventeen

1. Vieregg, Brenda Jones. "Exploring Eldercare." News Hour with Jim Lehrer Transcript, December 24, 1999. Available online on PBS Website www.pbs.org/newshour/bb/health/july-dec99/eldercare.

2. Landy, Karen and Buettner, Linda. "Communicating with Your Care Receiver." The Caregiver Manual and Caregiver Guide for Southwest Florida. Florida Gulf Coast University Website. www.fgcu.edu/cfpa/manual.

Day Nineteen

1. Adapted by permission from a speech given by Catherine Davis, February 28, 2004, Delta Kappa Gamma Area X Luncheon, Fort Worth, Texas.

Day Twenty-Three

2. Brzowsky, Sara. "How To Be Stress-Resilient." Parade Sunday Newspaper Magazine, October 12, 2003, p. 12.

Day Twenty-Four

1. Crawford, Dan R. *Night of Tragedy, Dawning of Light*. Colorado Springs, Colorado: Shaw Books, 2000, cover.
2. Davis, Verdell. *Let Me Grieve But Not Forever*. Dallas: Word Publishing, 1994, p. 4.

Twenty-Five

1. Banks, Carolyn. "Aging in Place Means Independence." LifeTimes, Blue Cross and Blue Shield of Texas Newsletter, January, 2004, p. 12.
2. Banks, p. 12.

Day Twenty-Six

1. Stanphill, Ira. "I Know Who Holds Tomorrow." Copyright 1950 by Ira Stanphill.

Day Twenty-Seven

1. Russell, Bob and Scott, Bobby. "He Ain't Heavy; He's My Brother." Published by Hollies Music, 1970.
2. Pek-san Lui and Nancy Martland. "Family Support: Siblings with Disabilities." Available online at www.tufts.edu/cfn/family-storystarter/fs-siblingsewithdisabilities.shtml, pp. 1, 4.

Day Twenty-Eight

1. Wexler, Nancy. "To Those Who Have Assumed the Role of Care-Giver." Getting It Right Newsletter, Issue 10, September, 2001. Available online at www.nancy-wexler.com.

Day Twenty-Nine

2. The Well Spouse Foundation Website. www.wellspouse.org.
3. "Caregiving for Spouses." Evergreen Commons Website. www.evergreencommons.org.
4. "Alone Is Not Lonely." Mainstay, The Well Spouse Foundation Website. www.wellspouse.org,
5. Abel, pp. 1- 2.

Day Thirty

1. "Tips for Family Caregivers." Erie County Department of Senior Services Website. www.erie.gov/depts/seniorservices/TakeControlofYourself, p. 1.

Day Thirty-One

1. Shantinath, Shachi D. "What to Do When You Feel Scared, Anxious or Excessively Worried." Caregivers' Center Website. www.healthandage.com, 2003.

Day Thirty-Two

1. Poem written by Sandra Winner, Fort Worth, Texas, for Sandra S. Webb on November 8, 1998. Used by permission.

Day Thirty-Three

1. Loosely based on "All I Need To Know, I Learned from My Cat" by Suzy Becker.

Day Thirty-Four

1. Abel, Barbara, p. 2.
2. "Mainstay Forum—Coping." Mainstay, The Well Spouse Foundation Website www.wellspouse.rog, p. 1.
3. "The New National Concern: Eldercare." Spring Lawn and Garden, The Star Group, March 2004, p. 3. 137

Day Thirty-Five

1. Gilliam, Larry. "Experience Reparenting: A Re-opportunity To Have A Happy Childhood" (Seminar presented in Irving, Texas, 2004).

Day Thirty-Six

2. Turk, Gary. "Look Up." Mutual Responsibility Website. http://www.mutualresponsibility.org/culture/look-spoken-word-lyrics-gary-turk.

3. Alpert, Jonathan. "Why We Need to Start Looking Up from Our Smartphones." Inc. Website. https://www.inc.com/jonathan-alpert/why-we-need-to-start-looking-up-from-our-smartphones.html.

4. Wexler, Nancy, p. 1.

DAY THIRTY-EIGHT

1. Warren, p. 221.

DAY THIRTY-NINE

1. Barron, Lauren. "There's Much To Learn in How We Say Goodbye." Baylor Magazine, March/April, 2003, p. 52. Used by permission of Baylor Magazine.

To order additional copies of CRISIS CARE CRISIS PRAYER: FORTY DAYS OF CARE AND PRAYER FOR THE CAREGIVER

Have your credit card ready and go to

www.amazon.com

or

www.Store.WorldwidePublishingGroup.com

www.ingramcontent.com/pod-product-compliance
Lightning Source LLC
Chambersburg PA
CBHW071500080526
44587CB00014B/2171